FAST FIT

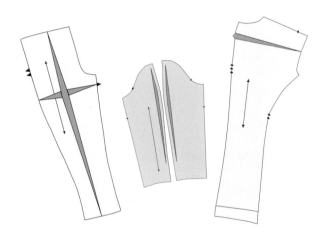

FAST FIT

Easy Pattern Alterations for Every Figure

SANDRA BETZINA

The Taunton Press

Publisher: JIM CHILDS

Acquisitions Editor: JOLYNN GOWER

Assistant Editor: SARAH COE

Editorial Assistant: MEREDITH DeSOUSA

Copy Editor: CANDACE B. LEVY

Indexer: CATHY GODDARD

Cover and Interior Designer: CAROL SINGER

Layout Artist: SUZIE YANNES

Photographers: SLOAN HOWARD AND JACK DEUTSCH

Illustrator: SHAWN BANNER

The Taunton Press
Inspiration for hands-on living™

Text © 2001 by Sandra Betzina
Photographs © 2001 by The Taunton Press, Inc.
Illustrations © 2001 by The Taunton Press, Inc.

Printed in Malaysia
10 9 8 7 6 5 4 3 2 1

The Taunton Press, Inc., 63 South Main Street,
PO Box 5506, Newtown, CT 06470-5506
e-mail: tp@taunton.com

Distributed by Publishers Group West

Library of Congress Cataloging-in-Publication Data:
Betzina, Sandra.
    Fast fit : easy pattern alterations for every figure /
Sandra Betzina.
        p. cm.
    Includes index.
    ISBN 1-56158-494-0
    1. Dressmaking--Pattern design. 2. Clothing and
dress measurements. I. Title.
  TT520 .B56 2001
  646.4'08--dc21   2001027029

To all of the people I love and all of the people who have loved me, making my life a banquet, full of joy and surprise.

Contents

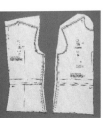

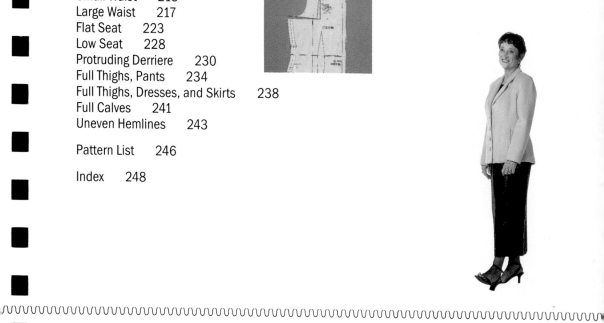

Introduction

No matter what our age, every body has distinctive bumps, lumps, and hollows. These bodily features are just one of the things that make us unique—but sometimes they can also present a challenge, especially when it comes to making garments that fit properly.

This book offers some innovative—and usually easy—adjustments to help you sew clothing with the best possible fit and, ultimately, the most flattering look.

There are many ways to alter a pattern. Consider pattern alterations an insurance policy for proper fitting. *Fast Fit* is full of the techniques that I have found successful and easy to do. Through lots of experimentation (which I've always been a big fan of) and the guidance of this book, you'll find yourself sewing up a storm of garments that will soon become favorites—clothes that fit are clothes you love!

Of course, my methods aren't the only ones that work. There are several fitting books on the market that use other fitting methods, and they may go into more detail for your particular problem. Here are some of them:

Pattern Making by the Flat Pattern Method, by Norma Hollen and Carolyn Kundel

The Art of Sewing–A Custom Fit, by Shirley Smith

Fitting and Pattern Alteration: A Multi-Method Approach, by Elizabeth Liechty, Delia Pottberg, and Judith Rasband

Bodymapping: The Step-by-Step Guide to Fitting Real Bodies, by Kathy Illian

Sewing for Plus Sizes, by Barbara Deckert

Fantastic Fit for Every Body: How to Alter Patterns to Flatter Your Figure, by Gale Grigg Hazen

The Sew/Fit Manual: Making Patterns Fit, by Ruth Oblander and Joan Anderson

Fit and Fabric, from *Threads* magazine

Part One

FITTING FACTS

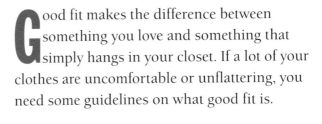

Good fit makes the difference between something you love and something that simply hangs in your closet. If a lot of your clothes are uncomfortable or unflattering, you need some guidelines on what good fit is.

WHAT IS GOOD FIT?

Good fit is a combination of two components: A garment must look good and must be comfortable. Although the concept of good fit varies depending on our different shapes and tastes, here are some criteria that can be used as a general guideline to determine whether a garment fits:

- Vertical seams are perpendicular to the floor.
  - Darts point to an area of fullness, end just before the full area, and have no pouch where they end.
- Shoulder seams are positioned at the shoulder joint, allowing a smooth fit over the upper chest.
- The garment back has some ease but no vertical or horizontal wrinkles.
- Sleeves don't bind or twist and don't have wrinkles that run across the cap or up and down.
- Necklines are comfortable. On a jewel neck, the front neckline rides just above the clavicle, and the back neckline is positioned where the clasp of a necklace sits.

- Waistline seams are not too tight or too loose and have no wrinkles under them or under the waistband.

- The hemline is even and parallel to the floor.

- Center front lines meet, which means that the garment is able to be buttoned without being overfitted.

- A dress or very fitted jacket with a high-cut armhole does not rise as the arm is raised. (Because of the ease in a looser-fit jacket or coat, raising the arm will cause the garment to rise as well, which is perfectly acceptable.)

These criteria may seem obvious, but they can sometimes be elusive when we put on a new garment and can't put a finger on why we aren't happy with it. As a result, a garment that does not fulfill most of these criteria is seldom worn. One of the biggest advantages to sewing is getting the right fit; so if you pay attention to these details, you'll end up with a closet full of "favorites."

YOUR BODY MEASUREMENTS

The first and most important ingredient for proper fit is your measurements. Every sewer I know has to make pattern alterations. But how can we ever expect to get patterns that fit without a set of up-to-date body measurements? If you take these once a year, you'll be able to make slight changes on your alterations and avoid those fitting disappointments.

How to Take Your Measurements

Take measurements in the same undergarments that you would normally wear under your clothes. Leotards, unless they are loose, tend to compress, making the results not totally reliable. Also avoid uncomfortable shoes, which can make you shift from side to side; instead, do without shoes for grounded measurements. Wearing a narrow belt or a length of 1-in. (2.5cm) wide elastic at the waistline and a small necklace helps the measurement process. As you wrap the measuring tape around you for each measurement, the tape should be snug without making an indentation.

FITTING TIP
Write your measurements on an index card to take with you when you buy patterns. The detailed numbers—your crib sheet—also come in handy during flat pattern alterations.

Dressing in a loose leotard or underwear is the only way to get realistic measurements. A narrow belt and a small necklace help define the waistline and the neckline, providing key points from which to take certain measurements.

PERSONAL MEASUREMENT CHART				
	My Measurements	Pattern Measurements	Alteration	Adjustment
High bust				
Full bust				
Cross chest				
Cross back				
Waist				
Shoulder width				
Bust point				
Back waist length				
High hip				
Full hip				
Upper arm girth				
Lower arm girth				
Sleeve length, full				
Sleeve length to elbow				
Cross back diagonals				
Waist to floor on left				
Waist to floor on right				
Crotch length, full				
Thigh				
Knee				
Pant length, full				
Pant length to knee				
Skirt length, short				
Skirt length, calf				
Skirt length, ankle				
Jacket length, high hip				
Jacket length, to crotch				
Dress and coat length				

IDENTIFYING FITTING PROBLEMS

Measurements are essential to the fitting process, but valuable information can also be gained simply from studying your body from all angles. For most people, it is difficult to do this objectively in the mirror. Instead, figure problems are easier to spot if you take three photos of yourself: one front view, one back view, and one side view. For these photos, wear a leotard (or underwear) and tie a string around your waist.

Without making judgments, study all three photos and ask yourself some questions. Your answers will play an important role in the fitting process.

- Do your shoulders slope? Is one shoulder higher than the other?

- How does your head sit on the body? Does it hang forward, creating uncomfortable necklines?

- Is your upper back rounded or flat? Is your back curved in quite a bit at the waist?

- Does your backside protrude or is it flat?

- Is one hip higher than the other? Is the hip curve gradual or does the fullness start very fast, right under the waist?

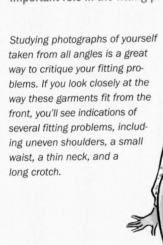

Studying photographs of yourself taken from all angles is a great way to critique your fitting problems. If you look closely at the way these garments fit from the front, you'll see indications of several fitting problems, including uneven shoulders, a small waist, a thin neck, and a long crotch.

- Does the tummy protrude?

- Do the thighs protrude at the side or in the front?

- Do the calves stick out farther than the backside when the knees are locked?

- Is there space between the thighs in the knee area?

- Is there a space between the thighs from knee to crotch?

Once you are familiar with your body, you can begin to identify your fitting problems. Then look for the relevant sections in Part Two of this book to find out how to alter your garments for the best fit in these problem areas.

Use the specific instructions below for taking each measurement, then record them on the "Personal Measurement Chart" (on p. 9) in the "My Measurements" column. It is useful to compare your measurements to the specific pattern measurements and to figure out how much a pattern should be altered for a good fit (see "Taking Flat Pattern Measurements" on p. 32). To help with this process, the chart also has columns labeled "Pattern Measurements," "Alteration," and "Adjustment" (see "All about Alterations" on p. 50), which will be referred to in later sections of this book. All these columns will eventually be filled in and can be used for easy reference later.

Where to Measure

There are a variety of measuring techniques that measure different parts of the body in different ways. If used consistently, just about any system is reliable; the following is the method I use to take my own measurements.

High Bust Measurement The high bust measurement is sometimes referred to as the chest measurement. It is taken above the bust, by placing the measuring tape high under the arm and higher than the bra band. This measurement is used to determine size for the big four pattern companies: Simplicity, McCall's, Butterick, and Vogue. (Other patterns use the full-bust measurement.)

The high bust measurement is taken across the upper chest, high under the arms.

The full bust measurement is taken around the fullest part of the bust, in line with the bra band in back.

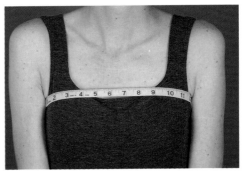

The cross chest measurement is taken above the bust, from crease to crease across the upper chest.

Full Bust Measurement The full bust measurement is taken around the fullest part of the bust and in line with the bra band in back. Next to the full-bust measurement, indicate your cup size. The full bust measurement is used to determine size when using patterns by Stretch and Sew, Quik Sew, Burda, New Look, Style, Neue Mode, Today's Fit (from Vogue and Butterick), and all patterns from small independent pattern companies.

Cross Chest Measurement The cross chest measurement is taken across the upper chest and above the bust from crease to crease, where the arms intersect the body. When this measurement is taken, your arms should be hanging at your sides. The measurement does not go completely under the arms but just from where the arms intersect the body. This intersection is where the front notch is located on your pattern.

Cross Back Measurement The cross back measurement is taken across the upper back from crease to crease where the arms intersect the body. Again, when this measurement is

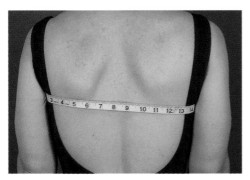

The cross back measurement is taken across the back from underarm crease to underarm crease.

The waist is measured by wrapping the tape firmly, but not too snugly, around the body. Check the measurement by sitting down.

taken, your arms should be hanging at your sides. The measurement does not go completely under the arms but just from where the arms intersect the body. This intersection is where the back notch is located on your pattern.

Waist Measurement The waist measurement is taken at the natural waist. (Do not try to measure over a belt or elastic band.) Take the measurement while standing; then sit down to make sure that a waist band made to that size would still be comfortable. Compare your waist measurement to that indicated on the pattern envelope for the size you are using. If the waist measurement doesn't match and your pattern is multisized, use a different size at the waist, blending gradually to the hip size.

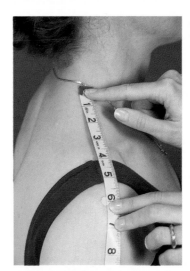

The shoulder width is measured from your natural neckline to the shoulder joint.

Shoulder Width The shoulder width can be determined only after the shoulder joint is located. To do this, lift your arm up and down. The point of connection between the arm and the shoulder is the shoulder joint. Mark the joint with a felt-tip pen. To determine shoulder

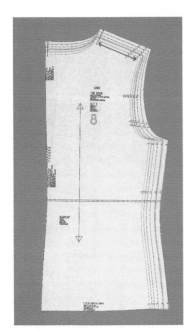

Compare your shoulder width measurement to that of the pattern, measured between seam allowances.

width, measure from the necklace you are wearing to the ink mark. Compare this measurement to the length of the shoulder seamline between the neckline and the armhole seam allowances on a pattern with a set-in sleeve. Any difference indicates narrow or broad shoulders.

Bust Point The bust point, sometimes called the apex, is determined by measuring from the middle of the shoulder to the nipple and between the nipples.

Bust points on patterns are often too high, so compare your measurements to those of your pattern to determine whether you need to lower, raise, or shorten the bust darts. To do this, divide your own between-the-nipples measurement in half; then on the pattern measure out this distance from the center front. Through this point, draw a vertical line from neck to waist. Now draw a line from the mid-shoulder to the vertical line. Pivot the ruler until the distance between mid-shoulder and the vertical line on the pattern

The bust point, or apex, is measured from the middle of the shoulder to the nipple (left). Also measure the distance between the nipples (above).

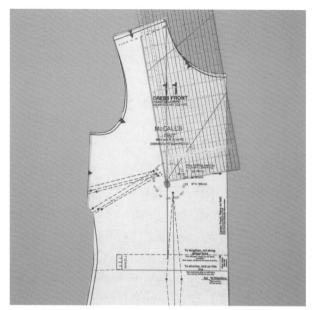

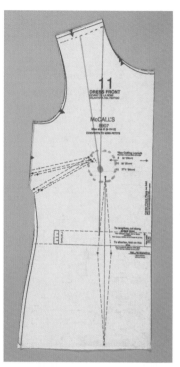

Find your bust point, or apex, on the pattern by first measuring the distance from mid-shoulder to the nipple on your body and then drawing that distance on the pattern.

Draw a 2-in. (5cm) diameter circle around the apex. Darts should point to but not enter this circle.

equals the distance from mid-shoulder to the nipple on your body. Mark an X on the pattern; this is the apex. Draw a 2-in. (5cm) diameter circle around the X.

Back Waist Length The back waist length is measured from the clasp on the back of the necklace you are wearing to the bottom of the belt or the elastic. Compare this to the back waist length indicated on the pattern envelope for the size you are using. Any difference indicates how much you need to lengthen or shorten the front and back bodice above the waist.

High Hip Measurement The high hip measurement, sometimes called the tummy measurement, is measured 3 in. (7.6cm) down from the waistline. Because the high hip is not usually stated on the pattern, take a flat pat-

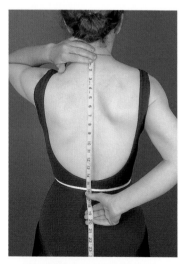

The back waist length is measured from the catch at the back of the necklace to the bottom of the elastic positioned at the waist.

The high hip or tummy measurement is measured 3 in. (7.6cm) below the waistline.

tern measure (see p. 32) in this area with the dart and pleats pinned closed, measuring between the seam allowances only. You'll need a minimum of 1½ in. (3.8cm) ease in this area unless you are very slim—then you can get away with ½ in. to 1 in. (1.3cm to 2.5cm).

Full Hip Measurement The full hip is measured around the fullest part of the hip (this position can be as low as your upper thighs). To determine how far down your full hip measurement is from the waist, measure down to this point from the bottom of the belt or elastic along the location of the side seam. Buy patterns for skirts and pants according to your full hip size.

Upper and Lower Arm Girths The arm girths are measured with the arm bent at a 45-degree angle. The upper arm girth is measured around the fullest part of the upper arm. Compare this to the pattern's arm girth measurement, which is taken around the sleeve between the seamlines, right under the armhole seam. You'll need 3 in. to 4 in. (7.6cm to 10.2cm) of ease at minimum here, unless you are using a knit, for which you need only about 1 in. (2.5cm).

If your forearms are large or small in proportion to the rest of your body, it's a good idea to take a measurement there as well. This is the lower arm girth measurement, which

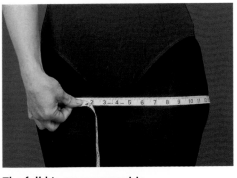

The full hip measurement is taken around the fullest part of the hip, even if it is down as far as the top of the legs.

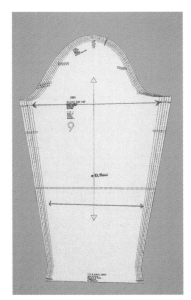

Compare your own arm girth measurements to those of the pattern, measured on both the upper and the lower arm between seamlines.

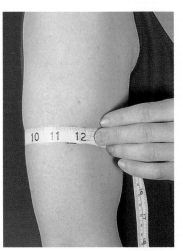

The upper arm girth is measured around the fullest part of the upper arm.

is taken at the fullest part on your lower arm between your wrist and elbow.

Sleeve Length, Full and to Elbow Sleeve length is measured with the arm bent. For full sleeve length measurement, measure from the ink mark at your shoulder joint to the top or bottom of the wrist bone, depending on where you like your sleeves to end. To determine whether you need to lengthen or shorten the sleeve on your pattern, measure from the dot at the seamline on the sleeve cap, which indicates shoulder seam placement, straight down to the hem crease of the sleeve. (Don't include the hem allowance in this measurement.) The difference is the amount you need to shorten or lengthen the sleeve.

The lower arm girth measurement is taken around the fullest part of the forearm.

The full sleeve length measurement is taken from the dot at the shoulder joint to the top or bottom of the wrist bone, depending where you want your sleeve to finish. The sleeve will hang ½ in. (1.3cm) longer when the arm is not bent.

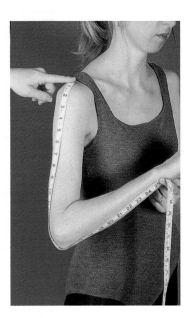 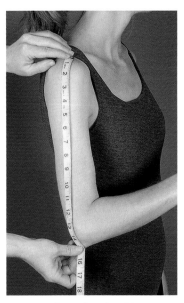

Measure from the shoulder joint to the elbow to determine the best location for an elbow dart or ease line.

Compare your own sleeve length measurement to that of the pattern, measured from the shoulder dot on the cap seamline down to the hem crease.

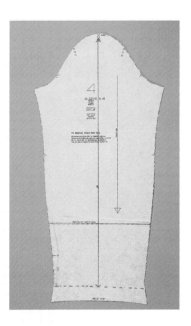

To find the proper location for any sleeve dart or easeline, measure the sleeve length to elbow, taken from the shoulder-joint ink mark to the elbow while the arm is bent. On your pattern, note the distance to the elbow dart if there is one. The difference is the amount you need to lengthen or shorten the sleeve above the dart or easeline.

Cross Back Diagonal Measurements The cross back diagonal measurements can tip you off to uneven shoulder heights and to how much they differ. Before you begin measuring, place a mark on the belt or the elastic (positioned at your waist) at center back, right at your spinal column. Measure diagonally from this point to the shoulder joint, marked in ink, on each side. Any difference between the two sides indicates a low shoulder and tells you how much lower it is; this is called the *low shoulder alteration amount*. This measurement may be difficult to take without a partner, but you can also determine alteration amounts when fitting the garment, for example, by sliding in extra layers of shoulder pads on the low side until all the wrinkles disappear.

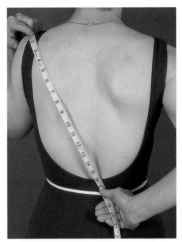

The cross back diagonal measurement is taken from the shoulder joint to the center back at the spinal column; be sure to measure both sides. A helper is a good idea for this one.

Waist to Floor Measurements The waist to floor measurements are taken on each side down the side seam to determine whether one hip is higher than the other. To take the measurement, put on a belt and slip a large paper clip on the end of the tape measure. Step on the paper clip on the end of the tape to measure each side up to the waist. The difference between the two sides will indicate how much should be added for a high hip.

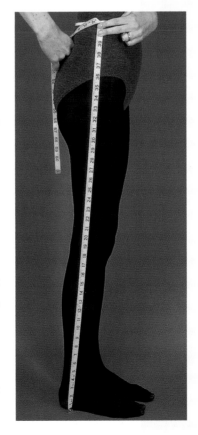

Crotch Length Measurement The crotch length measurement is taken through the legs with the tape measure against the body. Measure from the bottom of the belt or elastic in the back,

The waist to floor measurement is taken by stepping on a paper clip attached to the end of the measuring tape. Measure from the floor to the bottom of the elastic.

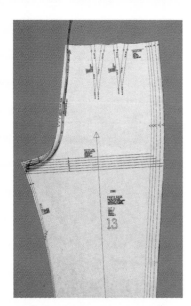

With the tape measure on edge, measure the pattern's front and back crotch lengths between seamlines.

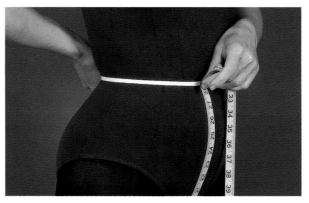

Measure the crotch from the bottom of the elastic in back, through the legs, to the bottom of the elastic in front.

FITTING TIP
Measure along seamlines by standing the measuring tape on edge, enabling it to go around curves.

which indicates the waist, through the legs to the bottom of the belt in the front. Add 1 in. (2.5cm) of ease to this measurement. Then divide the length so that the back crotch measurement is 2 in. (5cm) longer than the front measurement. Compare these lengths to the pattern by determining the front and back separately, measuring from the waist to the intersection of the crotch and the inner leg seam.

Lengthen the front and back of the crotch by only the shorter amount needed, which is the amount common to both. For example, if the front crotch needs to be lengthened ½ in. (1.3cm) and the back crotch 1 in. (2.5cm), lengthen both the front and back crotch pieces by ½ in. (2.5cm), the shorter amount, or the amount common to both. The additional ½ in. (2.5cm) needed on the back crotch will be added either to the back inner leg or at the waistline; you can split the amount and add a little at each place.

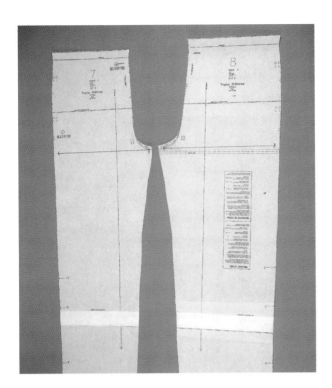

Compare the thigh measurement of your favorite pants to that on the pattern, measured between seamlines.

Measure the thigh when sitting down, with the tape positioned against the crotch while circling the leg.

Thigh Measurement The thigh measurement is taken sitting down, with the measuring tape positioned at the crotch and circling around the leg. Compare this to front and back flat pattern measurements taken horizontally between the seamlines at the crotch point.

FITTING TIP

Ease amounts vary, depending on style. Measure some of your favorite pants in the thigh and knee areas to see how much ease you like.

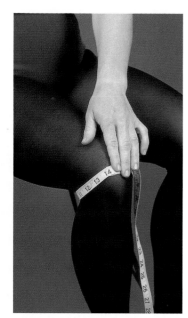

The knee measurement is taken around the bent knee.

Knee Measurement The knee measurement is also taken sitting down, with the leg bent. A minimum of 2 in. (5cm) ease is needed here.

Pant Length, Full and to Knee The full pant length measurement is taken down the side seam from the waist, either to the bottom of the ankle bone or to the floor (if you like to wear your pants long). Take this measurement in bare feet. Another technique is to measure your favorite pair of pants from the bottom of the waistband to the hem crease. Compare this measurement to the finished pant length stated on the back of the pattern envelope, and you'll know how much to shorten or lengthen the pant pattern before you cut.

The pant length to the knee is taken down the side seam from the waist to the middle of the knee. This measurement is helpful when shortening or lengthening pants. Mark the knee on the front of your pant piece. On the pattern, the knee location is halfway between the full hip opposite the crotch point and the hem crease at the bottom of the pants; your knee location may be higher or lower.

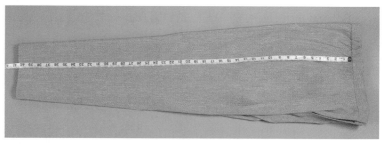

One way to determine a good finished pant length is to measure your favorite pair of pants at the side seam, from the waistline to the hem crease.

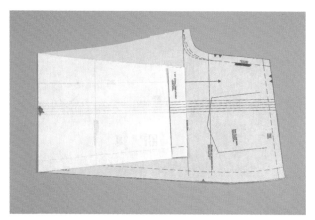

To determine the knee location on the front pattern piece, fold up the hem allowance, then fold the pattern piece so that hem crease is in line with the full hip, opposite the crotch point.

Find your knee location by measuring from the bottom of the elastic to mid-knee, at the approximate location of the side seam.

Skirt Length Measurements In addition to the above measurements, three skirt lengths should be taken:

- Just above the knee, if you wear short skirts; if not, then just under the knee.

- Mid-calf; or, if your calves are large, low calf.

- Above the ankle.

Compare these to the finished lengths stated on the back of the pattern envelope and you will know how much to shorten or lengthen the pattern before you begin cutting.

Jacket Length Measurements Jacket length measurements are taken at the center back, from the clasp on your necklace to the desired finished jacket length. Jackets hemmed to the high hip length and to just below the crotch length can be worn by all figures. Compare your desired measurement to the finished

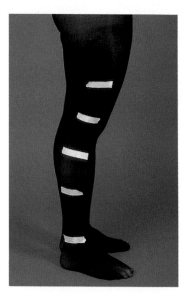

It's useful to have a variety of skirt lengths on hand. Put the tape at the bottom of the elastic and measure the different skirt lengths.

Two jacket lengths are taken: one to the high hip (for a shorter jacket) and one to just below or above the crotch (for a longer one).

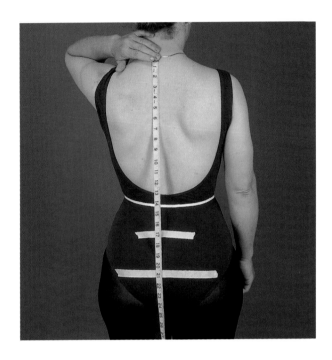

length on the back of the pattern envelope to determine how much to shorten or lengthen the jacket before you start cutting.

Dress and Coat Length Measurements Dress and coat lengths are taken at the center back, from the clasp on your necklace to the finished length you prefer. Compare the measurement to the finished length stated on the back of the pattern envelope to determine how much to shorten or lengthen before you cut.

After you've taken all these measurements, you'll have a good idea where you need to adjust your pattern. The information that follows will help you nail down the exact numbers for your pattern alterations.

BUYING THE RIGHT SIZE

Coming up with a realistic pattern size is an important step, one that I emphasize in all my classes. But all too often a sewer measures herself, then refuses to use the right pattern size. A little voice says, "I can't be that big." But remember—a size 12 in ready-to-wear translates into a size 16 in a home sewing pattern. It doesn't make you any bigger; the sizes simply aren't compatible. The fact is, pattern size has no relation to your ready-to-wear size, so don't try to compare them. In other words, don't let a larger size get in the way of a good fit.

Once you get home from the fabric store, you will not have access to the pattern sizing chart, supplied in the back of the pattern books. Thus I have provided one for you on p. 26. Each company has its own measurement chart, but all the charts are very close, if not identical. The charts printed here were supplied by Butterick Company, which means they work for Butterick and Vogue patterns.

How to Choose a Pattern

If you're buying a pattern for pants or a skirt, choose the pattern size by your hip measurement. If you're buying a pattern for a jacket, top, or dress, buy the pattern based on the high bust or full bust measurement, depending on which company makes the pattern. It's best to use the high bust measurement for Butterick, McCall's, Simplicity, and Vogue because these patterns tend to run large in the upper chest. Today's Fit by Sandra Betzina is one exception in Vogue and Butterick. For Today's

MEASUREMENT CHART

Misses'/Misses' Petites

Misses' patterns are designed for a well-proportioned and developed figure, 5 ft. 5 in. to 5 ft. 6 in. (1.65m to 1.67m) without shoes. Misses' Petites patterns are designed for the shorter figure, 5 ft. 2 in. to 5 ft. 4 in. (1.57m to 1.62m) without shoes.

	X-Small		Small		Medium		Large		X-Large		XX-Large
Size	6	8	10	12	14	16	18	20	22	24
Chest	28½"	29½"	30½"	32"	34"	36"	38"	40"	42"	44"
Bust	30½"	31½"	32½"	34"	36"	38"	40"	42"	44"	46"
Waist	23"	24"	25"	26½"	28"	30"	32"	34"	37"	39"
Hip	32½"	33½"	34½"	36"	38"	40"	42"	44"	46"	48"
Back waist	15½"	15¾"	16"	16¼"	16½"	16¾"	17"	17¼"	17⅜"	17½"

Reprinted with permission from Butterick Company.

Today's Fit

Today's Fit patterns are designed for the changing proportions of today's figure, about 5 ft. 6 in. (1.67m) without shoes. The waist and hips are slightly larger than Misses' and the shoulders are narrow.

Size	A	B	C	D	E	F	G	H	I	J
Bust	32"	34"	36"	38"	40½"	43"	46"	49"	52"	55"
Waist	26½"	28½"	30½"	32½"	35"	37½"	41½"	44½"	47½"	50½"
Hip	34½"	36½"	38½"	40½"	42½"	45"	48"	51"	54"	57"
Back waist	15¾"	16"	16¼"	16½"	16¾"	17"	17¼"	17¼"	17¼"	17¼"

Reprinted with permission from Butterick Company.

Women's/Women's Petite

Women's patterns are designed for the larger, more fully mature figure, 5 ft. 5 in. to 5 ft. 6 in. (1.65m to 1.67m) without shoes. Women's Petites patterns are designed for the shorter woman's figure, 5 ft. 2 in. to 5 ft. 4 in. (1.57m to 1.62m) without shoes.

	X-Small		Small		Medium		Large		X-Large		XX-Large
Size	14W	16W	18W	20W (38)	22W (40)	24W (42)	26W (44)	28W (46)	30W (48)	32W (50)
Bust	36"	38"	40"	42"	44"	46"	48"	50"	52"	54"
Waist	29"	31"	33"	35"	37"	39"	41½"	44"	46½"	49"
Hip	38"	40"	42"	44"	46"	48"	50"	52"	54"	56"
Back waist	16½"	16¾"	17"	17¼"	17⅜"	17½"	17⅝"	17¾"	17⅞"	18"

Reprinted with permission from Butterick Company.

WORKING WITH EASE

Ease is the extra amount of fabric needed beyond the body measurement to get the look on the pattern envelope. Movement ease is the base minimum of fabric added so you can move and sit. Design ease is the fabric added to give the garment "style." Ease is added into the pattern but should not be added into the body measurement.

Ease may vary from 2 in. (5cm) in a very fitted garment to 20 in. (51cm) in a very loose garment. The amount you decide to include in your garments is largely based on personal preference, or whether you like your garments to be very fitted or a bit loose. Once you understand the concept of ease, you will no longer be surprised by garments that are overfitted in your problem areas.

Fit, Stretch and Sew, Quik Sew, Burda, New Look, Style, and Neue Mode, as well as patterns from independent pattern companies, buy your size according to the full bust measurement. If the pattern is described as very loose fitting and you are under 5 ft. 6 in. (1.6m), use a size smaller pattern than your measurements indicate. Both the proportions and the size of the shoulder will be more flattering.

Ease and Your Pattern

The pattern description on the back of the envelope gives a hint of how much fabric beyond the body measurements has been added to create the style. For example, if a shirt is described as "semifitted," it will have 4 in. to 5 in. (10.2cm to 12.7cm) of fabric beyond the body measurement for the size you are using. On the other hand, if the blouse is described as

> **FITTING FACT**
> If you have a large tummy, a looser fit over the hip yields a better silhouette, making the hip look more in proportion.

"loose fitting," it will have 5 in. to 8 in. (12.7cm to 20cm) of fabric beyond the body measurements. For exact numbers, look at the "Ease Chart" (above on the facing page). "Sandra's Personal Ease Preferences" (below on the facing page) lists the amount of ease I like in my own garments.

EASE CHART

Silhouette	Bust Area			Hip Area
	Dresses, Blouses, Shirts, Tops, and Vests	Jackets (lined or unlined)	Coats (lined or unlined)	Skirts, Pants, Shorts, Culottes
Close fitted	0" to 2⅞"	Not applicable	Not applicable	0" to 1⅞"
Fitted	3" to 4"	3¾" to 4¼"	5¼" to 6¾"	2" to 3"
Semifitted	4⅛" to 5"	4⅜" to 5¾"	6⅞" to 8"	3⅛" to 4"
Loose fitted	5⅛" to 8"	5⅞" to 10"	8⅛" to 12"	4⅛" to 6"
Very loose fitted	Over 8"	Over 10"	Over 12"	Over 6"

SANDRA'S PERSONAL EASE PREFERENCES

Pants and Skirts

	Tummy	Hip	Thigh
Trousers with darts, pleats folded out	1" to 1½"	1"	4" to 5"
Fitted pant	½"	2"	2" to 3"
Full pull-on pant	6"	6"	5" to 6"
Narrow pull-on pant	1" to 2"	2" to 3"	3"
Straight skirt	½"	2"	
Bias skirt	4" to 5"	4" or more	
A-line skirt	1"	3" to 4"	

Tops, Dresses, Jackets, and Vests

	Bust	Tummy	Hip	Sleeve Girth
Semifitted top	3"	3"	3"	2" to 3"
Overblouse	6" to 8"	6" to 8"	6" to 8"	3"
Straight dress	2½"	3" to 4"	3" to 4"	1" to 1½"
Fitted jacket	4"	4"	4"	3"
Boxy jacket	5"	5"	5"	1" to 1½"
Coat	6" to 8"	3" to 4"	3" to 4"	1" to 1½"
Vest	4" or more	4" or more	4"	

KNIT PATTERNS IN WOVEN FABRIC

You finally found the perfect pattern for a fabric you love, when you notice a notation on the pattern that states "for knits only." Can this pattern be made in a woven fabric? In most cases, yes. Although there are a few differences to be aware of, the primary difference between a pattern drafted for knits and one drafted for wovens is the ease factor.

Ease and Fabric Stretch

If you want to make the pattern in a woven, ease must be added in. To determine how much, look at the stretch factor listed on the back of the pattern envelope. Double knits and single jerseys have a slight stretch factor, between 18 and 20 percent. Moderate stretch knits such as velour, stretch terry, and sweater knit have a 25 to 35 percent stretch factor. Super-stretch fabrics such as spandex knits and ribbing have a 75 to 100 percent stretch factor. If the pattern suggests a fabric with slight stretch, add ¼ in. (6mm) at all side seams, including the sleeve. For moderate stretch, add ½ in. (1.3cm); and for super stretch, add 1 in. (2.5cm).

When making blouses, add ease at the underarm sleeve seams to correspond to the amount you added at the side seams. The armhole on the bodice

front and back must also be lowered by ½ in. (1.3cm) and then blended back into the original armhole line just above the armhole notches, so that a smooth curve results. Sleeve cap ease has also been reduced for knits. Add it back in by raising the sleeve cap by ⅜ in. (1cm) and widening the sleeve cap by ⅛ in. (3mm) on each side. A pretest of the sleeve is always a good idea.

Other Adjustments

There are other differences between a pattern for knits and one for wovens. On a knit pattern, darts are nonexistent, lengths are shortened, and necklines are raised. Knit patterns are also shorter, because knit fabric relaxes over time, lengthening the garment slightly. To account for this, add

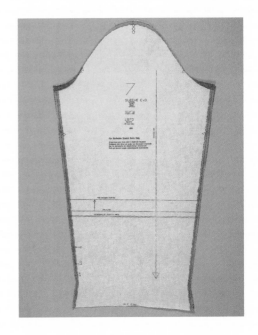

When adding ease on blouses, remember to add ease at the underarm sleeve seams, to lower the armhole, and to raise and widen the cap.

½ in. to 1 in. (1.3cm to 2.5cm) length back into the pattern for the bodice, sleeve, skirt, and pants, depending on how much the knit stretches. If you are making pants, lower the crotch ½ in. (1.3cm) after adding the suggested amounts at the side seams. If the pant legs are narrow, add ¼ in. (6mm) to the front inner leg. Darts and pleats on the pants are usually eliminated and replaced by an elastic waist. Front necklines must also be lowered ¼ in. (6mm) and then blended into the original neckline halfway up the neck toward the shoulder.

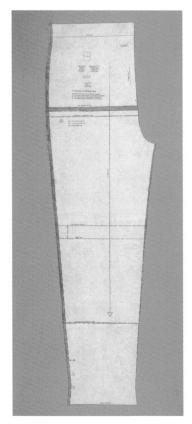

To make pants from woven fabric using a knit pattern, add ½ in. (1.3cm) at the side seams and lower the crotch. If the pant leg is narrow, slightly increase the width at the inner leg.

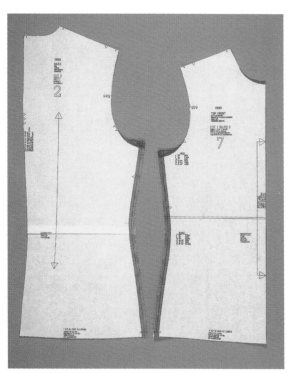

A pattern designed for knits can be used for wovens by adding ease at the side seams. Armholes and necklines should also be lowered.

TAKING FLAT PATTERN MEASUREMENTS

Flat pattern measurements are measurements of the pattern pieces in certain key areas, such as the tummy, bust, and hip. Because everyone carries her fullness in different places, it is important to make sure the pattern is big enough across the tummy and the hip, in particular, to be both comfortable and flattering.

A flat pattern measurement tells you how much room a finished garment will have, rather than how much you hope it has. This is especially helpful if one area of your body is oversize in proportion to the rest of your body. For example, if you know your tummy is large in proportion to the rest of you, always take a flat pattern measurement of the tummy area. Or, if a full bust is your problem, make it a habit to take a flat pattern measurement of the bust area. Full hips get the same treatment.

The key to success is remembering that seam allowances aren't included in the measurements, and neither is anything that extends past the center front, since the garment meets at center front if buttoned or zipped. Darts and pleats are folded out so these are not included in the measurement either, because they will be sewn closed.

Measuring the trouble spots takes a few minutes, but think of the frustration and disappointment you're avoiding. Without flat pattern measuring, you are truly gambling. The finished garment might fit—or it might not.

> **FITTING FACT**
>
> It isn't necessary to cut out the pattern pieces to take measurements, but I find it easier to work on the cut-out shapes. If possible, leave several inches of pattern paper outside the cutting lines on the side seams of each pattern piece so that you can add on at the side seams before cutting out.

Measuring Your Pattern

Once you get the hang of flat pattern measuring, it becomes second nature. The following instructions take you step by step through a process that can be repeated for all patterns. Depending on the garment's design and the number of pattern pieces, you may be compiling measurements from several pattern pieces to come up with a number that corresponds to a problem area on your body. For example, if your jacket pattern has a front, side front, side back and back pieces, all four pieces should be measured to come up with a total measurement that corresponds to your bust measurement.

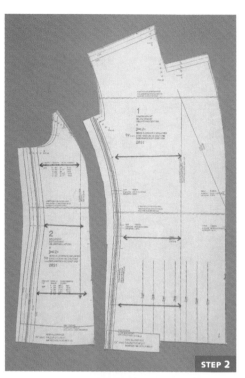

STEP 2

Measure across the front from seamline to center front through the middle of a bust dart or, if the pattern has no dart, 2 in. (5cm) below the armhole cutting line.

1 Highlight your size or sizes on your pattern pieces, making smooth transitions between sizes.

2 Measure the full bust. Place all of the front bodice pattern pieces on a flat surface. Working on each piece separately, place a ruler across the pattern so that it's perpendicular to the grainline and runs through the middle of the bust dart. If the garment doesn't have a bust dart, take the measurement 2 in. (5cm) below the bottom of the armhole cutting line. Measure from one side seam to the center front or foldline, excluding the seam allowances and extensions past the center front. If the pattern has a side front piece, measure its width at the bustline and add it to the front

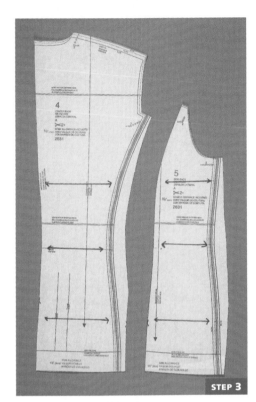

Take the back width measurement at a location that corresponds to the front width, usually 2 in. (5cm) below the armhole cutting line.

pattern measurement. Double the final number to obtain the bust front measurement.

3 To get the total circumference of the bust on the pattern, you must also measure the back bodice piece. Place all of the back pattern pieces on a flat surface. Working on each one separately, place a ruler across the pattern so that it's perpendicular to the grainline and the same distance below the armhole as it was when you measured the front pattern piece. Measure from one side seamline to center back or foldline, excluding the seam allowances. If the pattern has a side back piece, measure its width at the same distance below the armhole and add it to the back pattern measurement. Double the final number to obtain the bust back measurement.

4 Add the back measurement to the front bust measurement from Step 2. This measurement falls along the same line that you use when you measure your body at the full bust.

5 Measure the high hip or tummy. For most women, the tummy measurement—3 in. (7.6cm) below the natural waist—tends to be a problem area and is often more important than the waist measurement. To take the flat pattern measurement of this area, collect the front and back pattern pieces. Draw a horizontal line across the pattern, 3 in. (7.5cm) down from the

waistline, with the ruler perpendicular to the grainline. If the garment is to be cut on the bias, simply draw a horizontal line across the pattern in the tummy area.

6 Fold out any darts or pleats, and pin them closed; pleats on pants are folded out to the crotch. If the pant has a slant front pocket, fold back the seam allowance on the front pattern piece in the pocket area. Match the dots for the side front and front in the pocket area, and overlay the pocket seamline with the pocket location line on the side front. Measure across each pattern piece from the seamline to the center front along the horizontal line. Add the measurements together. If the front and back are cut from the same pattern pieces, then double the number to obtain the garment's finished tummy measurement.

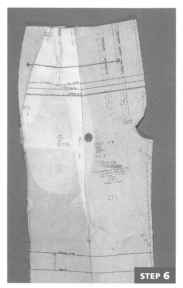

STEP 6

To measure the pattern's high hip area, pin out darts and pleats. For pockets, slide the side front into position, matching the pocket placement dots.

7 Measure the front full hip. A flat pattern measurement for the hips is taken at the place on the pattern that corresponds to the fullest part of your hips. For example, if you are widest 10 in. (25.4cm) below the waist, measure at the side seamline 10 in. (25.4cm) down from the natural waistline marked on the pattern. (Don't include the seam allowances.) Measure the back at the full hip in the same way; then add the front and back measurements. If the front and back are cut from the same pattern pieces, double the number to get the total flat pattern measurement. Waistline shaping makes the distance between the waistline and the center front shorter than the waistline and the same location at the side.

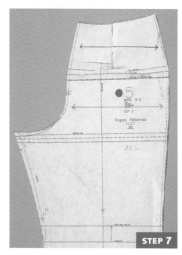

STEP 7

Measure the full hip with darts folded out, between the seamlines at tummy and full hip locations.

CLOSET COMPARISONS

Once you have the flat pattern measurements in hand, you need to compare them to your body measurements, which can be tricky. Movement and design ease need to be taken into consideration. This is a good time to use the clothes that are already in your closet—they can help you make new garments that fit well and minimize figure problems. Whether you're making a new jacket, skirt, vest, or other garment, use the clothes in your wardrobe as templates.

**FITTING
FACT**

To save fabric, the industry uses ⅜-in. (1cm) seam allowances everywhere, except on the neck and the collar, where ¼-in. (6mm) seam allowances are used for ease in sewing and to eliminate trimming. Pattern companies use ⅝ in. (1.5cm) seam allowances everywhere.

We all have garments we wear over and over again because they are both comfortable and flattering. Duplicate these by taking a few measurements to eliminate the guesswork and ensure success for your next project. Even the sewing failures stuck in the back of the closet can be useful; figuring out why a garment did not work can help you avoid making the same mistake twice. With the dimensions of your favorite garments in hand, you can alter your new pattern to match. To draw up a master plan for your alterations, measure the garment following the instructions below.

How Your Favorites Measure Up

With pattern, pencil, and tape measure in hand, head for your closet. Pull out clothes that are similar to the type you want to make. For example, if your next project is an overblouse (one that is worn on the outside of a skirt or pants and is not tucked in), start with a favorite overblouse in your wardrobe.

STEP 1

To duplicate the fit of a favorite piece from your closet, measure the garment at the bust, tummy, and hip.

1 Button or zip up the garment; place it on a flat surface and smooth it out as much as possible. On a top, measure the bust, tummy, and hips. For pants, measure the tummy and hip areas, plus the leg circumference at the hem. Since you are measuring the garment flat, double this measurement to obtain the entire circumference of the garment.

Take a flat pattern measurement from the center front to the side seamline and from the center back to the side seamline. Add the amounts together and multiply by two to get the measurement all the way around the body.

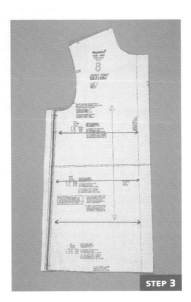

STEP 3

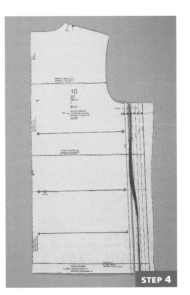

STEP 4

Make your curves as smooth as possible so they'll lie flat when pressed.

2 Put on the garment and take an honest look at how it fits. If any location is a little tight or loose, add or subtract a few inches to the garment measurements that you noted in Step 1.

3 Highlight your size on the pattern pieces, then take a flat pattern measurement of each piece at the bust, tummy, and hips. Measure from the center front to the side seamline and from the center back to the side seamline. Because pattern pieces represent only half of the garment, multiply each measurement by two.

4 Compare the flat pattern measurements to the finished garment measurements with any desired adjustments. A difference between the numbers means you need to add to or subtract from the pattern's side seam at that loca-

> **FITTING TIP**
> Tape your measurement index card to the wall so it doesn't get lost. Hiding the card behind a picture keeps your measurements private!

BIAS-CUT GARMENTS

If you've had any experience sewing bias-cut garments, you know that they tend to hang closer to the body, sometimes revealing areas we might prefer to camouflage. The truth is, you don't have to be tall and skinny to wear clothes cut on the bias, but you do need to have enough ease to allow for the relaxing of the fabric. As a result, sewing techniques for bias-cut garments call for extra ease and wider seam allowances.

On my own garments, I usually add 5 in. (12.7cm) of ease to my tummy measurement, then compare it to the pattern measurement. While 5 in. (12.7cm) may seem like a lot, the nature of the bias will reduce this amount drastically, resulting in about 2 in. (5cm) of actual ease. Add, from waist to hem, whatever amount it takes to get 5 in. (12.7cm) of ease at the side seams.

Wider seam allowances of 1½ in. to 2 in. (3.8cm to 5 cm) are also necessary. Without them, the seams stretch as they are sewn and tend to ripple. If the width of the pattern seam allowance is only ⅝ in. (1.5cm), add an additional 1⅜ in. (3.5cm) to all cut vertical seam edges. Then you can sew 2-in. (5cm) seams without any rippling. To allow the seamlines to relax along with the bias fabric, sew seams with a narrow zigzag (0.5mm width and 2.5mm length). Taking these precautions is worth the time—you'll definitely wear the next bias-cut garment you make!

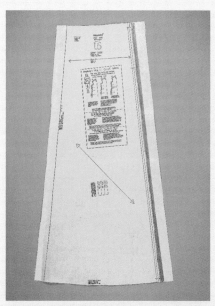

Bias-cut garments need more ease and wider seam allowances to eliminate ripply seams and give a flattering fit.

tion. In a different color pen, draw new cutting lines to indicate the alteration; taper the new cutting lines and seamlines back to the originals where pattern alterations aren't needed. Curves that are too extreme will not lie flat when pressed, so refine your curves with a hip curve until they are smooth.

THE FITTING SHELL

Sewing a garment entails a fair amount of money—and time—so why gamble on fit? Pattern companies can help, and some offer a tool for just that purpose: a fitting shell.

Every company develops its patterns with a particular body shape (and its corresponding measurements) in mind. Those "typical" measurements are then turned into a basic pattern called a *block* that, in turn, is the starting point for every garment designed by that particular company. (This is a case where brand loyalty counts!) A fitting shell is, in essence, the basic

FITTING TIP
Make a shell from an unforgiving fabric, such as muslin, 1-in. (2.5cm) gingham check, or a firm striped denim. On your body, garment lines shift off the horizontal and vertical wherever you have a fitting problem, which is why a checked fabric is ideal.

This is a typical fitting shell for Vogue patterns. A fitting shell can be used to customize fashion patterns to your figure.

block plus movement ease. If you make up the shell and put it on, any place where your body differs from the basic block will be quite apparent. Armed with this information, you'll already know the adjustments you need to make to every pattern you buy from that company.

Of course, you wouldn't want to wear a fitting shell out of the house; as a rule, it'll be downright ugly. Even if it's a perfect fit, it'll be so snug that you won't be able to completely bend your elbows. Still, I highly recommend making one. This important exercise highlights problem areas, so that you can work out alterations to use on every pattern from that company. A shell cannot be used as an overlay to superimpose on other patterns; style ease is added to the fashion pattern but not to the block, so trying to trace the block features onto any other pattern simply won't work.

If you have two favorite pattern companies, consider making a fitting shell for both. Or, if your favorite doesn't have a shell, make one yourself using a pattern with a set-in sleeve and a waistline seam that fits close to the body. If you can't find a fitted dress pattern with a waistline seam, use the most fitted dress you can find.

If your favorite pattern company does not provide a fitting shell, use a fitted dress with a waistline seam to make your own shell.

FIT INSURANCE

For those times when it seems as if your entire life were on fast-forward, try a bit of "fit insurance" before getting started. The idea behind fit insurance is to cut wider seam allowances—on side seams only—for a bit of fitting forgiveness. You might be tempted to follow industry standards and use ⅝-in. (1.5cm) seam allowances on the side seams; however, if you haven't pretested the pattern, you're taking a chance. Instead, why not add an extra ⅜ in. or 1 in. (1cm or 2.5cm) to the side seams of a bodice, skirt, pants, and sleeves? You can add ⅜ in. (1cm) and baste in 1-in. (2.5cm) side seams, or add 1in. (2.5cm) and baste in 1⅝-in. (4cm) side seams.

To take advantage of the wider seam allowances, machine-baste the side seams together using a contrasting color for the bobbin thread; then try on the garment. No matter how well you altered the pattern, the fabric might influence the way the garment pieces hang on your body. Because most garments need a little tweaking here and there to get the look you want, basting the seams together offers an easy way to make changes.

Fit insurance is a shortcut to pretesting every pattern in scrap fabric. It not only saves time but could also save you from troublesome fitting problems later.

Add 1 in. (2.5cm) at the side seams and baste together at 1⅝ in. (4cm). Think of the garments you could have saved if only they had wide seam allowances that could be let out.

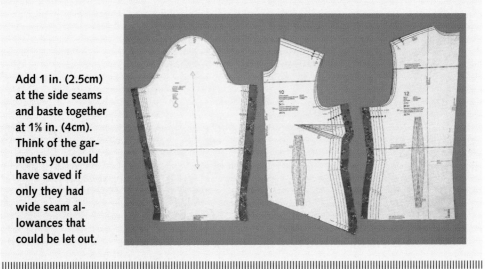

Making a Fitting Shell

Before you begin, make sure you have an accurate set of your body measurements in hand. It's likely that your size is not consistent throughout your body. Since most fitting shell patterns are multisize, use the size that corresponds to your body in each area.

1 To make personalized cutting lines, trace the size in each area of the garment that matches your measurements. Make smooth transitions between sizes, using a curved ruler if you need help. If you're uncertain about what size to use in the upper chest and upper back, use a tracing wheel to copy two or three possible sizes onto your fitting shell fabric (see "Altering Multisize Patterns" on p. 58). If you need a larger size at the waist, transition gradually from your upper body; it's best to start 2 in. (5cm) below the armhole cutting line. An abrupt size shift near the tummy gives you a fabric bulge.

2 Alterations are easier to make with a bit of extra fabric at the sides. Cut out the garment pieces using 1½-in. (3.8cm) side seam allowances. Use ¼-in. (6mm) neck seam allowances and stick to the standard ⅝-in. (1.5cm) allowance everywhere else. If you suspect a problem in the shoulder area, use 1½-in. (3.8cm) seam allowances there as well.

3 Before you start sewing a fitting shell, it's important to use a tracing wheel to mark all of the sewing lines for your size, as well as the center front, on your garment pieces.

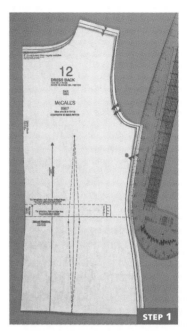

STEP 1

Find a matching curve on a curved ruler to help blend size changes gradually and smoothly.

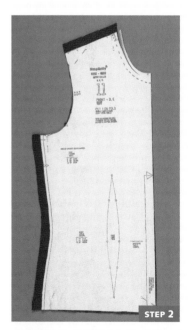

STEP 2

Wider seam allowances allow you to alter with a lot less hassle.

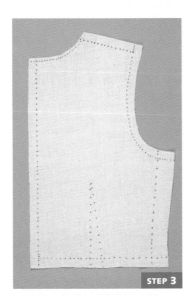

STEP 3

Mark all the sewing lines on your newly cut-out shell.

FITTING TIP

If you're ever tempted to skim a little bit off your measurements, try measuring your body with the metric numbers on your tape measure facing out. Then flip the tape over for the equivalent in inches—a sobering experience!

4 Machine-baste the dress together. Stay-stitch the neckline and clip through the neckline seam allowance at 1-in. (2.5cm) intervals. Don't bother inserting a zipper at center back. Instead, put on the garment and bribe a companion to pin the garment together along the center back seamline. If you can't find help, sew up center back and make the garment opening at center front, so that you can pin the closure by yourself.

5 Look in the mirror. Don't be discouraged! If the garment is too tight at the hips, waist, or bust, let out the side seams until the fit is comfortable. (This is when those wide side seams come in handy.) Now look for other fitting problems. Start at the upper chest, getting the fit you want in the neck and shoulders first. In most cases, garment wrinkles point to the problem. Adjust shoulders, sleeves, and other trouble spots, removing the basting and re-pinning as necessary. If you can't eliminate all of the problems, cut out a new shell, adjusting for your problems before you cut out the garment pieces.

6 Check the dart point on the bust dart—it should end 1 in. (2.5cm) back from the bust point. For smaller busts, the dart point can end ½ in. (1.3cm) away.

7 When you're happy with the fit, remove the shell and run a permanent felt-tip pen along the seamlines. Take the shell apart, and trace the new seamlines onto the pattern pieces. Draw new cutting lines with ⅝-in. (1.5cm) seam allowances.

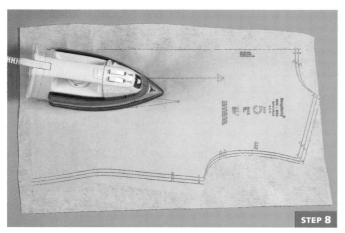

STEP 8

Stabilizing pattern pieces makes it easier to use them for future reference. Fuse each piece to interfacing, glue side up.

8 Stabilize the back of the pattern pieces by applying Fuse-A-Shade or Pellon interfacing to the wrong side. To do this, lay the interfacing on a pressing surface with the glue side up. Overlay the pattern piece onto the interfacing so that the wrong side of the pattern piece is against the glue side of the interfacing. Starting in the middle, use a dry iron and press out toward the edges. Having stabilized the pattern pieces, you can now reference them for adjustments on other patterns from the same company. Store them rolled on a paper towel holder or tack them on the wall in your sewing room.

After you have determined your alterations by making a fitting shell, you can make the same alterations on all future patterns from that company. Because each pattern is designed from the basic block, any problems that showed up on the fitting shell will show up on other styles unless you make alterations.

> **FITTING TIP**
> Baste with a contrasting thread color so it's easy to see the basting thread when it is time to remove it.

PRETESTING A PATTERN

Pattern pictures can be misleading; to waste expensive fabric on a so-so style is very disappointing. If your fabric is expensive or the construction time is long (such as for a tailored jacket), pretesting the pattern in scrap fabric is a great idea. Not only can you work out any fitting problems but you can also determine if the style is worth making.

Fabric you've had stashed for more than three years is perfect for making a pretest gar-

This pretest—marked with center front, button openings, and pocket location—was made from leftover fabric in my stash. For the least amount of work, you can pretest just half of the garment.

This pretest jacket is made from a variety of different scrap fabrics. Because the hem and sleeve edge allowances were folded up before cutting, the raw edges represent the finished lengths. Pattern markings are visible for center front, collar, pockets, and buttonholes. A collar isn't necessary on a pretest garment.

It's not imperative that you make a pretest for every garment, but they are particularly valuable if:

- You are using expensive fabric.
- You are making more than 12 adjustments.
- You are trying a pattern brand that you rarely use.
- Your last three patterns were failures
- The finished garment—a coat or jacket, for example—takes more than 10 hours to make.

ment. At this point, it's likely that a pretest is the only hope left for using the material!

After altering the pattern, but before cutting out the fashion fabric garment pieces, make up the garment in this inexpensive or disposable material. You can eliminate all of the styling details in the pretest, such as pockets and collars, and choose to cut just the main pieces and one sleeve. The extent of your pretest garment is up to you. In less than an hour you'll know exactly how the finished garment will look on you. You can now decide if the pattern is worth making or should be simply tossed in the trash. Getting rid of a $20 pattern and some old fabric is a lot less painful than spending an entire day on something that turns out to be a disappointment.

Making a Pretest

Pretesting a pattern is down-and-dirty sewing, so set aside any perfectionist tendencies. Try on the pretest garment, critique the fit and style, then simply toss the pretest in the trash.

> **FITTING TIP**
> Steer clear of muslin for a pretest; it does not drape like most garment fabrics, so you won't get a realistic idea of the finished garment's appearance.

1 Choose a disposable or inexpensive fabric that has the same drape as the fashion fabric. Knits on the sale table at a fabric store are perfect for pretesting a pattern that you intend to sew up in a knit fashion fabric.

2 Fold up all the hems on your pattern pieces so that your pretest shows the finished garment length.

3 Carefully cut the major garment pieces from the pretest fabric, transferring all marks and notches. Be sure to mark the center front, center back, darts, waist, buttons, buttonholes, and pockets; the center front marking is very important, because you will pin center fronts together to check the fit. Don't bother cutting out facings, collars, and pocket pieces. The cut edge of the fabric is the finished length of the garment and sleeves. Machine-baste the pretest with a contrasting thread color. Press the seam allowances and darts flat. Ignore all of the finishing.

4 Put on the pretest, pinning it together at the center back or center front opening. Stand back and critically assess the way it looks. (Try to ignore the ugly pretest fabric.)

- Inspect for wrinkles that indicate a fitting problem.

- Look at the shoulders. Try several shapes and thicknesses of shoulder pads, to see if any improve the garment's appearance.

- Check for enough ease at the bust and hips. If you're pretesting a coat or

---

FITTING TIP

I mark center front, buttonholes, and pockets with tailor's tacks, so that I can see the markings when I try on the pretest.

---

jacket, try on the pretest with garments underneath.

- Carefully assess the back fit to ensure it isn't too narrow or wide.

- Check the finished length of the garment and the sleeves. If you decide to shorten the garment length, raise the pocket to maintain pleasing proportions. Don't move the pocket above the high hip, or more than 2 in. (5cm) down from the waist.

- Are the darts, buttonholes, and pockets nicely positioned? I like a buttonhole between the breasts. A button opening ½ in. (1.3cm) above or below the waist is more flattering than one exactly at the waistline. Also, make sure that center front button and buttonhole marks match exactly.

Is the garment worth making? Are you really excited about it, or are you indifferent? Unless the shape and style thrill you, don't waste time on this pattern. If, on the other hand, you love the design, note the changes you uncovered in the pretest then go ahead and alter the pattern. Now you can sew without any doubts, knowing in your heart that the garment is a winner.

Never feel guilty about tossing a pattern—only 50 percent or so are really worth making. A pattern that doesn't progress past a pretest doesn't count as a failure. In fact, you should count it as a win, because you didn't waste time or a great piece of fabric.

> **FITTING TIP**
> **Cardinal Rule of the Bulge:** Do not overfit if you have any bulges you want to hide.

All about Alterations

The beauty of sewing your own clothes is that they can be made to fit your body perfectly, thanks to alterations. Once you have taken your body measurements and identified your fitting problems, you're finally ready to alter the pattern. Keep reading to find out the process of making alterations as well as how to remedy some of the most common pattern problems.

SEQUENCE FOR PATTERN ALTERATIONS

The process of altering a pattern can be confusing without a master plan. Because most people make anywhere from five to eight pattern adjustments, a sequence must be followed to save the integrity of the style and to avoid confusion. In addition, an alteration in one area may affect another area. For example, shortening the bodice or crotch affects the finished length, so it makes sense to adjust the length after shortening in other areas. It's a good idea to familiarize yourself with the proper sequence of pattern alterations before going any further with altering a specific pattern. The steps below will take you through the correct order in which to make alterations to a multisize pattern. (If your pattern is not multisize, skip Steps 1 and 2, and make notes about areas in which you may need to add or subtract according to your own measurements.) It's not likely you'll need to make all of these adjustments, but understanding how one change affects another will make your alteration process much easier.

1 In the pattern envelope, find the sheet that lists measurements for all sizes. Circle the size you need for different parts of your body.

2 Using a highlighter pen, outline the cutting line for the size or sizes you will be using for different areas of your body. Make smooth transitions between sizes.

3 Shorten or lengthen the distance between the bottom of the armhole and the shoulder, if necessary. Make the identical alteration in the sleeve cap.

4 Compare your back waist length to the back waist length listed on the size you are using. (If you altered between the bottom of the armhole and the shoulder, take this into account.) Shorten or lengthen the front and back bodice, if necessary.

5 On pants, shorten or lengthen the crotch on the front and back, if necessary.

6 Compare the finished length on the back of the pattern envelope to the length you want. Shorten or lengthen the pattern accordingly within the body of the garment (not from the bottom) to preserve the integrity of the style. If you shortened anywhere in the bodice or crotch, take this into account.

7 If the sleeves are either too short or too long, alter the sleeve length now.

FITTING TIP
Remember that Burda patterns are ½ in. (1.3cm) shorter in the crotch than other patterns.

8 If your sleeves are often too tight, check the sleeve girth. A jacket sleeve is most comfortable if it measures 3 in. to 4 in. (7.6cm to 10.2cm) larger than your arm. A dress in a woven fabric needs 2 in. (5cm) of ease and a knit, 1 in. (2.5cm) of ease. Alter sleeve width, if necessary.

9 Check sleeve cap ease to see whether you should reduce it for a smoother effect. If your sleeves often have a vertical wrinkle, add ½ in. (1.3cm) in height to the sleeve cap.

10 If you are narrow in the shoulders, change the width now. If you used a size smaller above the armhole when outlining your multisize pattern, there's no need to make this change.

11 If you have a broad back and need alterations in this area, make them now.

12 Make alterations for sloping or square shoulders next.

13 If your garments ride too low in the back, make alterations for a rounded back now.

14 Make neckline changes if your necklines ride too high or too low or are too tight or too loose.

15 Make collar changes if necklines or shoulders have been altered.

16 To accommodate a large or small bust, make changes in dart positioning and sizing as well as princess seam changes.

ONE-SIZE PATTERNS

One-size patterns are few and far be-tween these days. But what do you do if you've just found a great pattern that's not multisize, but your body defi-nitely is? The answer is to buy accord-ing to the full bust size. You can always make pattern alterations if you are small in the upper chest (see "Narrow Upper Chest" on p. 181 or "Small Bust" on p. 163). And if your hips are large in proportion to the rest of your body, or you are not sure if you need to add at the hip, first compare your hip measure-ment to the hip measurement on your pattern. The difference between your body measurement and the stated pat-tern measurement is the total alteration amount. Divide this number by four to determine the adjustment to each side seam. Add these numbers to your "Per-sonal Measurement Chart" on p. 9.

17 If your waist is small, increase the size of the darts and pleats. If your waist and tummy are large, add to the side seam at the waist and high hip. Plan to take out any re-sulting fullness by easing along the waistline.

18 If your hips are larger than the pattern you are using, add to the side seam all the way to the hem.

19 Next, make swayback reductions or scoop out the center back waistline if your pants and skirts wrinkle under the waist.

20 If you are making a skirt or pants and you have a tummy, add height above the waist at the center front.

21 If you are making pants and you have full thighs, add to the pattern at the front inner leg seam.

22 If your backside protrudes and your pants ride too low at the center back waist, add to the back inner leg seam.

23 If you are making pants and your backside is flat, outline a size smaller on the back inner leg.

24 If you have bow legs or knock knees, cut the pattern apart horizontally under the crotch, lengthen on one side and shorten on the other.

25 If none of your jackets or vests buttons because of a large tummy, take a flat pattern measurement this area and make sure that the pattern is big enough before you cut. You can always cut a bigger size in this area.

WHERE TO BEGIN

After you have taken your measurements and entered them onto your "Personal Measurement Chart" (p. 9), you're ready to take the first steps toward altering the pattern. Follow the instructions below and you'll be on your way to garments that are both comfortable and flattering.

BODY MEASUREMENTS

MISSES'/JEUNE FEMME

SIZE/TAILLE	6	8	10	12	14	16	18	20	22	24
Bust	30½	31½	32½	34	36	38	40	42	44	46
Waist	23	24	25	26½	28	30	32	34	37	39
Hip	32½	33½	34½	36	38	40	42	44	46	48
Bk. Waist Lgth.	15½	15¾	16	16¼	16½	16¾	17	17¼	17⅜	17½
T. de poitrine	78	80	83	87	92	97	102	107	112	117
T. de taille	58	61	64	67	71	76	81	87	94	97
T. de hanches	83	85	88	92	97	102	107	112	117	122
Nuque à taille	39.5	40	40.5	41.5	42	42.5	43	44	44.5	45

STEP 1

Compare your body measurements to the size numbers listed on the instruction sheet of your pattern.

Altering the Pattern

1 Look up the measurements on the pattern size you're using. This information is found on the pattern envelope and in the measurement chart at the back of the pattern catalog. List this information in the "Personal Measurement Chart" under "Pattern Measurements."

2 Subtract the pattern measurements in the second column from your body measurements listed in the first column. This is the total amount of alteration needed; enter this amount in the "Alteration" column in the chart. Do the same for every row in the chart. You will not be able to complete the chart until all of your fitting problems have been identified by making a garment pretest.

USING CURVED RULERS

If you have difficulty drawing smooth curves and cutting lines, French and hip curves are helpful. To smoothly connect new lines with the original cutting lines, use the part of the curve that lines up with the markings you are trying to connect. For example, for alterations on the front armhole, use one part of the

French curve from the notch up, and another part of the curve from the notch down, as shown below. French curves are helpful for neckline and armhole changes, and hip curves work well for additions and subtractions between the waist and the hip and for changes above the waistline.

French and hip curves help make fast-and-easy sizing adjustments.

French curves are perfect for armhole and neckline changes.

Hip curves are best for the hip and waist area.

MAKING WIDTH ALTERATIONS

Not all bodies are equal size in the front and back. As a result, you may want to alter more at either the front or the back side seams. A woman with a large bust or tummy, for example, may need three quarters of the total alteration at the front side seam and only one quarter at the back side seam.

If you know you're proportionally larger in front or back, you can make all of the adjustment to the front or back side seams. Patterns with more seams, such as side front and side back, are better if you need to add a lot in one particular area, because the pattern can be expanded in smaller increments.

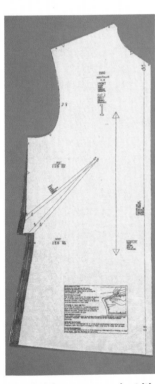

Decide where you need width the most: front or back. If you are proportionally larger in the front, make all or most of your pattern alterations on the front side seam.

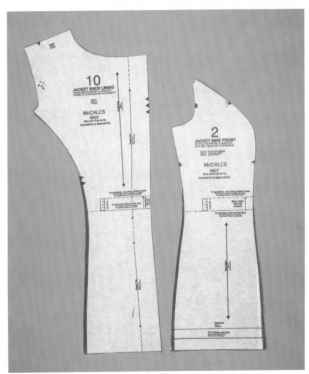

Patterns with more pieces allow larger alterations to be made more subtly.

Armhole and Sleeve Adjustments

Any side seam alteration that affects the armhole must be transferred to the sleeve. Additions on the sleeve to accommodate the larger armhole should be smoothly tapered back to the original cutting line. After adding to the sleeve, check the sleeve balance by matching the underarm seams. If the sleeve twists and will not lie flat when you pin the sleeve seams together, you may be tapering too quickly. To fix this, change the cutting lines on the underarm seams. To keep the circumference the same, you can add to one side of the sleeve and cut off from the other.

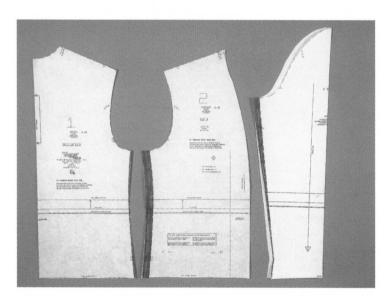

A sleeve addition is needed to accommodate this side seam alteration, which has affected the armhole.

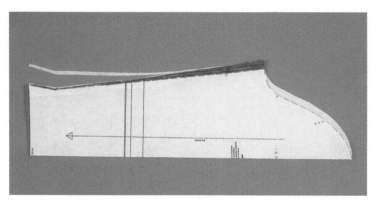

Changing the underarm seams may be necessary if the sleeve has been thrown off balance as a result of an alteration.

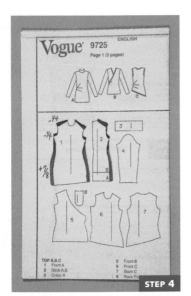

STEP 4

Drawing a mini version of your planned pattern alteration helps give an overall view of what you're trying to accomplish.

3 Divide the total alteration measurement by four to get the amount that each side seam should be altered. Pattern width adjustments are made at the four side seams rather than at center front or center back, which would affect the neckline and shoulder width. Note this number in the "Adjustment" column of your "Personal Measurement Chart."

4 To draw your planned alterations, use the pattern piece sketches on the pattern layout page in your envelope.

Now that you have a good idea of what needs fixing, the next step is to make those adjustments on the pattern itself. If you have a multisize pattern, follow the instructions below. If not, indicate where adjustments are needed at the side seams.

ALTERING MULTISIZE PATTERNS

Assembling a garment is like putting together a puzzle: Each piece can be a different size, as long as the matching pieces fit together at the edges. Multisize patterns take away some of the pressure of buying exactly the right size for every portion of the body. For example, if the lower half of your body is larger in proportion to the top half, you can use the smaller size on top and the larger size on the bottom.

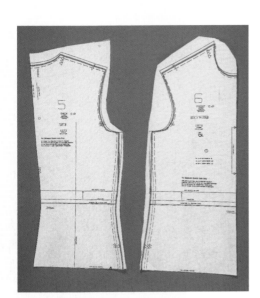

This bodice indicates a larger size at the waist and high hip area, with a smooth transition made between the larger and smaller sizes.

The easiest way to begin making your alterations is to work with the sizes listed on your multisize pattern. The following steps will get you started on the process of customizing it to your body shape and measurements. When you've finished tracing out the sizes you think you are in multisize, refine the pattern further by consulting individual fitting problems in the second part of this book. Because altering for a broad back is one of the most common alterations, I focused on it here specifically.

Altering Multisize Patterns for Tops and Dresses

When making the alterations on your pattern, use a highlighting marker to trace the cutting lines and a French curve, a hip curve, or a straight ruler to ensure smooth transitions between sizes. After the first fitting, you can refine the cutting lines by making changes with a permanent felt-tip pen.

1 Make length adjustments first, starting with the back waist length. Compare your back waist length measurement to the back waist length measurement for the size you are using on the back of the pattern envelope. Lengthen or shorten accordingly.

2 On the bodice front below the armholes, trace the cutting lines for your full bust size. Continue tracing the cutting lines above the armholes, unless you have a narrow upper

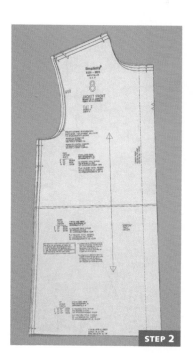

STEP 2

Trace cutting lines for the full bust measurement from the armhole to about 3 in. (7.6cm) down, where you can begin transitioning to a larger size if necessary. If you have a narrow upper chest or shoulder, use a size smaller than the bust size above the front armhole.

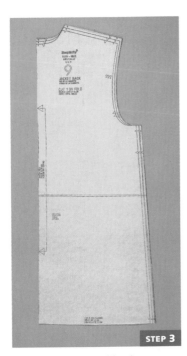

STEP 3

If you have a broad back, you may end up with a size 12 armhole in the front and a size 16 in the back.

chest or narrow shoulders. In this situation, use a size or two smaller in the armhole only. You do not want to change the height of the armhole or the size of the neck.

3 Choose cutting lines for the bodice back that best suit your back width. A broad back needs a larger size on the back armholes; a narrow back requires a smaller size above the armholes. Use the same neck and shoulder cutting line as you did on the front; only the back armhole is changed to increase the back width.

4 For the sleeve cap, use the same size as the bodice front armhole and transition to the same size as the bodice back; start the transition at the dot on the armhole that marks the

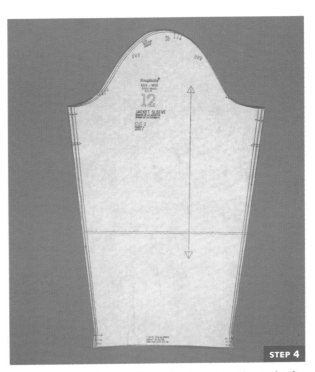

STEP 4

A sleeve cap can be one size in front and another in back. Make a smooth transition between the sizes at the dot that marks the shoulder seam.

FITTING FACT

Always measure and alter the length before the width. If you measure and alter the width first, the bust point, natural waistline, and hip location on the pattern may no longer correspond to your body.

shoulder position at the top of the sleeve cap. For the underarm sleeve cutting line, use the size that corresponds to the bodice side seam.

5 If the back bodice is enlarged, the front and back shoulder seam lengths won't match; ease them to fit. For medium-weight fabrics, run an easeline on the back shoulder. Heavier fabrics don't ease well, so you may need to add a small dart to make the back shoulder the same length as the front (the same can be done if your front is very narrow compared to the back). Center a 3-in. (7.6 cm) long dart on the back shoulder seam. The base of the dart can be ⅜ in. (1cm) wide, or whatever it takes to make the front and back shoulder the same length.

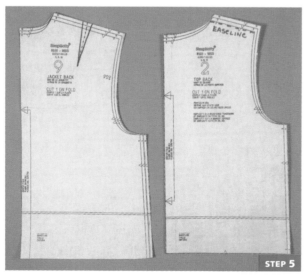

STEP 5

To make a larger back fit a smaller front at the shoulders, run an easeline on the back shoulder or add a small dart, depending on the weight of the fabric you're using.

> **FITTING TIP**
>
> If you're using a lightweight fabric and are easing different front and back shoulder lengths to fit, pin the beginning and end of the front and back shoulder seam allowances together. Stitch them together with the longer shoulder closest to the feed dogs.

MULTISIZE DILEMMA

What size should you buy if your bust fits into one multisize group and your hip fits into another? If you are making a garment that includes both the bust and the hip (as for a dress), buy the multisize pattern according to your full bust measurement. Then compare your full hip measurement to the largest size on the pattern that fits your bust. The difference between these two measurements is the amount of the total alteration. Divide by four and add this amount to each side seam.

For example, after you buy the pattern to match your full bust measurement, you note that your full hip measurement is 3 in. (7.6cm) bigger than the largest size in the envelope. Divide the difference by four to get ¾ in.

(1.9cm), which is the amount you need to add to the side seams at the outside hip of the largest size in the envelope. From the neck to the bust, about 2 in. (5cm) down from the armhole, cut the size that fits your full bust measurement. Then begin transitioning out to ¾ in. (1.9cm) beyond the cutting line at the hip for the largest size, only at the side seams. Cut out for the largest size on all other seams at the hip. If you are small in the upper chest, cut a size smaller above the armholes.

If the pattern must fit only the waist and hip (as for pants) or bust and waist (as for a blouse), buy the pattern that fits your full hip measurement or full bust measurement. Then alter the waist as explained on p. 215 or p. 217.

Altering Multisize Patterns for Pants and Skirts

1 Make length adjustments first. If necessary, alter the crotch length for pants, then alter the finished pants or skirt length.

2 Trace the cutting lines for the hip from the fullest part of the hip to the finished length of the pants or skirt. On pants, use the same size as the hip on the inner leg seam.

3 If your legs are short, use a smaller size on the lower leg of pants at the inner and outer leg seams. Begin the transition between sizes at the knee.

4 If you have a flat bottom, cut a size larger at the back inner leg seam.

5 If you have full thighs, cut a size larger at the front inner leg seam.

UPSIZING AND DOWNSIZING

Not everyone fits into the sizes offered by pattern companies. If you are smaller than a size 8, or larger than a size 16, your pattern selection is extremely limited. The information in the following sections allows you to downsize or upsize any pattern to fit your body.

Petite Downsizing

Patterns for sizes 4 and 6 are few and far between. Some styles can be special ordered, and companies are responding to the "smaller" market with petite-fit and adjustable pattern options. But sometimes we simply fall in love with a pattern that isn't available in our size. If you're petite and have trouble finding patterns in your size, try sizing down an 8 with a few alterations.

Essentially, downsizing involves reducing the length and width of a garment and, in some cases, shortening the sleeves of the bodice and lower body pattern pieces. A smaller pattern is also graded smaller (downsized) at the neck and armholes, but these areas are already so small on a size 8 that you don't need to bother with them. In general, a size 8 pattern needs be made smaller above the waist; however, most patterns don't need the reduction below the waist (thanks to unrealistic pattern sizing).

The same vest is shown here on an average-size woman and, sized down, on a petite woman. Not only is the vest itself smaller throughout the body but the styling elements have also been sized down, including the pockets and the collar.

1 For downsizing alterations, work from the smallest size on the pattern pieces. On the bodice front, draw a vertical line between the shoulder and the waist. To reduce the pattern by one size, draw a parallel line ¼ in. (6mm) away from the first; to reduce it by two sizes, place the second line ½ in. (1.3cm) away from the vertical line.

2 To adjust the pattern above the waist only, make a cut into the pattern from the side seam at the waist to the second vertical line. Then, using the two vertical lines, make a fold

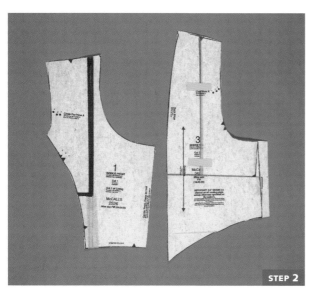

STEP 2

This bodice is being downsized only above the waist by making a vertical fold from the shoulder to the waist. A cut from the side seam into the alteration lines allows the pattern piece to flatten.

in the pattern by bringing one line over to the other. Tape it in place and smooth out the cutting lines.

3 If you're short, reduce the bodice length between the armhole and the neck. The easiest way to figure out the correct amount to shorten the bodice pattern piece is to try on a finished pattern-size 8 garment and fold out the excess fabric on the garment until the armhole is in the right place. The fit is correct when the garment lies flat against the upper chest without wrinkling. Measure the amount that was folded out to determine the amount of your alteration.

4 Draw a horizontal line on the front bodice above the armhole notch, perpendicular to the grainline. Make another line parallel to the

first, distancing it the amount that you want to reduce. Fold the second line to the first and tape it in place. Make the same adjustment on the back pattern piece.

5 Fold out the same amount on the sleeve cap, right above the notches (see "Short" on p. 79).

6 When shortening a pattern below the waist, never take more than 2 in. (5cm) off the bottom of a pants, skirt, or dress hem—doing so distorts the garment shape. Instead, fold out 1 in. or 2 in. (2.5cm or 5cm) in different locations until you're happy with the length. Tape the folds and then true the irregular side seams by drawing a straight line and cutting off the excess tissue (see "Altering Length" on p. 71).

Although measurements and comparisons are helpful, making a pretest of the downsized pattern is the only way to tell if you have accomplished the desired results. Use scrap fabric, eliminate facings, and insert only one sleeve; in less than 30 minutes you'll have a good idea of whether or not your proposed alterations will actually do the trick.

Upscale Sizing

Full-figured women often experience the same disappointments as petite women when it comes to fashion-forward patterns—they simply don't come in their size. But just because you are larger than a size 16 doesn't mean you don't want your choice of patterns.

Although there is a limited selection for larger sizes, there are patterns available to fit

---

FITTING TIP

The extra time it takes to make a pretest is well worth the effort. Once you figure out the adjustments that work for you, you can repeat the same alterations on all of your patterns of the same size made by that pattern company.

Upsizing a garment involves more than just adding fabric at the side seams. All of the styling elements must be upsized to be in proportion to the rest of the garment.

FITTING TIP
Today's Fit patterns in the Vogue pattern book are sized A to J, rather than numerically, and go up to a 55-in. (140cm) bust and a 57-in. (145cm) hip. The patterns are multisize and the upper chest is smaller; the back is wider; and the sleeves, waist, and tummy areas are roomier than in other patterns.

your figure, including Today's Fit from Vogue and Butterick. But if you still need alterations, don't worry. A fabulous garment is within your grasp, and the alterations won't take nearly as much effort as you might expect.

As always, taking good body measurements is of prime importance, even if you're working from a plus-size pattern. Take waist, tummy, and hip measurements sitting down, add the recommended garment eases from the "Up-scale Figure Ease" chart on p. 68, and compare

UPSCALE FIGURE EASE	
Garment	**Movement and Design Ease**
Jacket	5" (12.7cm) at bust; 6" to 8" (15.2cm to 20.3cm) at hips
Overblouse	8" to 10" (20.3cm to 30.5cm) at hips
Straight skirt	3" (7.6cm) at hips
Full pants	10" (25.4cm) at hips
Tailored pants	4" (10.2cm) at hips
Narrow pants	3" (7.6cm) at hips

these measurements to the flat pattern measurements. Keep in mind that full figures expand differently and need more ease, according to fit expert Gale Grigg Hazen, author of *Fantastic Fit for Every Body*. Refer to the chart to determine how much ease should be added for various types of garments. These measurements are current, based on research and fit tests conducted by Vogue Patterns for the Today's Fit collection.

Making a fitting shell in a plus size will tell you what changes to make when you *start* with a plus-size pattern. But suppose you want to make a pattern that is not even offered in a plus size?

As a pattern increases in size, the pattern is graded with small additions all over, not just at the side seams. For this reason, upsizing a pattern involves more than simply adding fabric at the side seams. Instead, the process involves superimposing the styling details of the smaller pattern onto a larger pattern, one that fits you. To do this, purchase the pattern you want to make in the largest size available, probably a size 16. Then go through your stash of plus-size patterns and find a similar style. If the jacket you want to make is boxy, choose a boxy style. (In other words, if the style you want to make is a loose overblouse, don't start with a fitted dress.) Then follow these instructions to start the alterations:

1 Lay the pattern pieces from the plus-size pattern on a flat table. Superimpose the pattern pieces from the pattern you want to make onto the larger ones.

2 Match center front and center back. Grainlines should be parallel but don't need to match.

3 To line up the shoulders and armholes, you may need to cut the smaller pattern apart vertically or horizontally. Draw a horizontal line across the pattern in the middle of the armhole, and draw a vertical line from mid-shoulder to the bottom of the garment. Cut the pattern apart and move the pieces so that the shoulders and armholes, as well as center front and center back, line up.

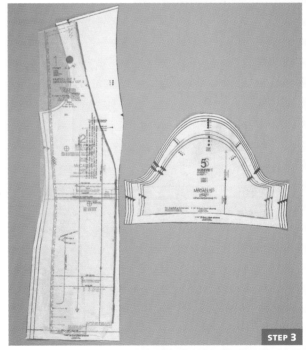

STEP 3

This sleeve overlay needs more than tweaking. Instead, use a sleeve that you know fits you.

4 Trace the style lines from the smaller pattern (lapels, pocket placement, and collars) onto the large pattern. If necessary, increase styling details such as the width of the collar

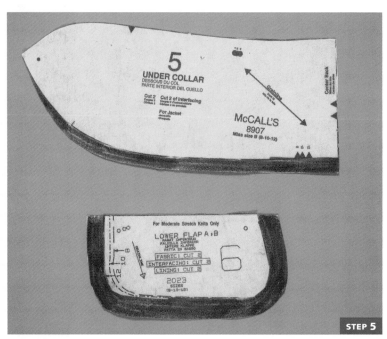

STEP 5

Collars and pockets need to be sized up to look in proportion to the larger size garment. Only the width of the collar is affected; keep the neck edge the same size.

and the length and width of pockets, to be more in proportion to your size; check the styling of these details against garments in your own closet. Use the sleeve from the larger pattern, because tweaking the sleeve here and there will not work.

5 Increase the width of the facing and collar pieces by ½ in. (1.3cm). Leave the neck edge intact.

6 Before cutting into your fabric, make a pretest from the newly altered pattern to refine the fit.

ALTERING LENGTH

Just as you have favorite garments that flatter and fit through the hips, chest, and shoulders, you probably also have ones that are the perfect length. Measure your favorite lengths, but keep in mind that garment length has a lot to do with proportion; make sure that the garments you choose are similar in shape to the one you plan to make. For more specifics on this alteration, see "The Length" on p. 76.

Garments that are too long are unflattering. Length must be altered within the body of the gament— not just at the bottom—to retain the original style and proportions.

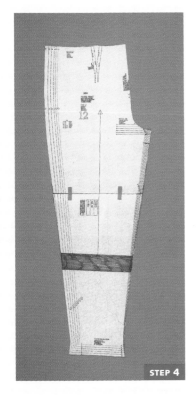

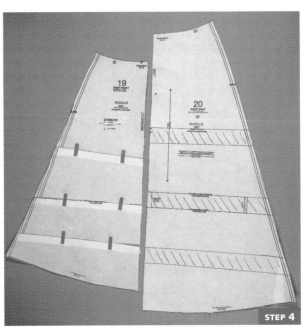

Lengthen pants and skirts both above and below the knee, to maintain the integrity of the style. Smooth out side seams with a long ruler.

STEP 4

1 Using a garment from your closet, measure its length on a flat surface. Depending on the garment, place the tape measure in these locations:

- *Coats, dresses, jackets, robes, and tops:* Center back at the base of the neck (where a necklace clasp rests) to the hem at center back.

- *Pants and skirts:* Along a side seam from the bottom of the waistband to the hem.

2 Try on the finished garment and assess the length. Do you want it shorter or longer? If so, add or subtract this amount from the garment length.

3 Compare your desired length to the finished length on the pattern envelope. The difference in these amounts is how much you need to alter the pattern piece.

4 Make your length alterations within the pattern piece to maintain the integrity of the style. Never make an adjustment larger than 2 in. (5cm) in any one spot.

To lengthen or shorten a skirt, draw lines across the pattern that are perpendicular to the grainline, unless the skirt is a bias cut. (For bias cut, simply draw a line across the pattern.) Cut the pattern apart along this line; to lengthen, add in strips of paper no wider than 2 in. (5cm). To shorten, fold out the excess no more than 2 in. (5cm) per alteration.

To lengthen or shorten pants, draw horizontal lines across the pattern, perpendicular to the grainline. Cut the pattern apart and extend the length by adding paper additions of no more than 2 in. (5cm) in each place to lengthen. To shorten, fold out the excess length in 2-in. (5cm) increments. Keep the grainline in a continuous straight line, and true up the cutting lines.

Now that you have a good understanding of your body measurements, your pattern measurements, and the changes you'd like to make, take a look at the appropriate sections in the next part the book to learn the details of making specific alterations. You're already well on your way to making better-fitting—and better-looking—garments!

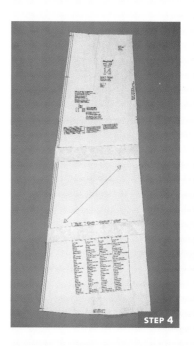

STEP 4

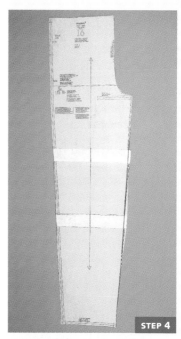

STEP 4

Rather than adding all the extra length to the bottom, lengthen within the body of the skirt or pants. Never add more than 2 in. (5cm) in any one place.

Part Two

PROBLEM AREAS

Fast Fit Solutions

Tall

THE PROBLEM

If the armholes on many of your garments often feel tight and as if they were placed too high, then you are long between the bottom of the armhole and the shoulder. It is common for tall or large women to feel like the armhole size needs to be adjusted. Patterns are designed for women who are 5 ft. 6 in. tall (1.65m), so if you are quite a bit taller than this average, adjustments must be made both above and below the armhole to give a garment the necessary balance.

Since people are usually tall or short proportionally, length must be adjusted not only from underarm to waist, and hip to hem, but also from the bottom of the armhole to the neck. Sleeves should be lengthened above and below the elbow shaping, and pants and skirt lengths must be adjusted at key points, listed below, to accommodate a full hip that is higher or lower.

FAST FIT SOLUTION

Lengthen the armhole by spreading it at the halfway point, and lengthen the sleeves both above and below the elbow. If you're making a skirt, extend or shorten your pattern piece according to your full hip, altering both between the waist and the full hip, and the knee to the hemline. For pants, spread the length addition over three locations throughout the garment.

STEP-BY-STEP SOLUTION

1 Locate the halfway point between the top and the bottom of the armhole on the front and back bodice and approximately the same spot on the sleeve cap. Draw a horizontal line through this point across the pattern, perpendicular to the grainline.

2 Cut the pattern apart along the horizontal line. Slide extra tissue paper behind the cut-apart pattern pieces; keep the pattern grainline in line when taping the pattern pieces back together. Smooth out the cutting lines in the armhole. You will need to lengthen between the armhole and waist as well.

3 Lengthen the sleeves above and below the elbow shaping. Standard locations for sleeve length alterations are the underarm to the elbow and the elbow to the wrist. Smooth out the cutting lines on the sides.

4 If you are tall, your full hip is either high or low. Extend or shorten your skirt pattern piece accordingly with an alteration between the waist and the full hip and between the knee to the hemline.

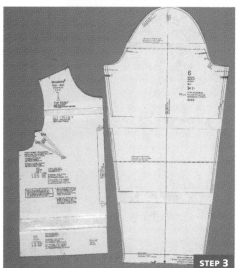

STEP 3

This bodice has been altered to add length at the armhole and within the body of the top. Sleeves have been adjusted at the sleeve cap, as well as in small amounts both above and below the elbow.

FITTING TIP
Tall people usually find that sleeves, jackets, pants, and skirts are all too short.

To accommodate a
high and low hip, this
skirt pattern has been
altered between the
waist and full hip
as well as below
the knees.

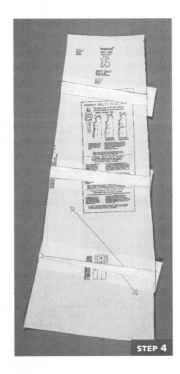

STEP 4

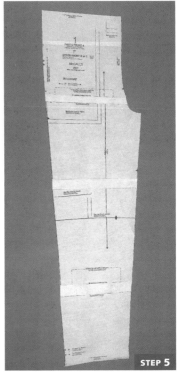

STEP 5

The three key points for lengthening pants: above the crotch,
between the crotch and the knee,
and between the knee and the
hem crease.

5 Lengthen pants in each of three key spots:
between the waist and the crotch point, the
crotch point and the knee, and finally the knee
and the hemline. Never shorten or lengthen
more than 2 in. (5cm) in any one spot. Altering
from crotch to waist will position the crotch
correctly; altering from crotch to knee posi-
tions the knee correctly, and altering from knee
to the hemline lengthens the lower leg. Alterations within the body of the pants maintain the
integrity of the style.

Short

THE PROBLEM

If you're shorter than 5 ft. 2 in. (1.57m), your garments may often end up with too much fabric between the armhole and the neck. As a result, necklines bulge and lapel and jacket fronts don't lie flat on the body. In addition, shorter women usually have shorter arms, and pants and skirt lengths may also need to be adjusted. If this sounds like you, don't worry, there's an easy to way to correct this problem with a few simple alterations on the front, back, and sleeve pattern pieces. Once your patterns are altered properly, your garments will be in proportion and, as a result, be much more flattering.

FAST FIT SOLUTION

Make a pretest to determine the correct amount to alter the bodice. On the front and back bodice pieces, fold out the desired amount above and below the armhole. Alter the sleeve cap by the same amount. Use your shoulder-to-elbow measurement to determine whether to shorten sleeve length either above or below the elbow shaping. If you are shortening the sleeve quite a bit—more than 2 in. (5cm)—you may need to shorten both above and below the elbow. To shorten pants or skirts, make small reductions over three locations throughout the body of the garment.

STEP-BY-STEP SOLUTION

1 Directly above the notches on the front and back bodice pieces, draw a horizontal alteration line across the back so that it's perpendicular to the grainline.

2 At the alteration line, fold out ¼ in. to ⅜ in. (6mm to 1.5cm), in effect, raising the armhole this amount.

3 At the corresponding location on the sleeve cap (directly above the notches), fold out the same amount that you altered the front and back. I suggest sewing up a pretest garment to make sure the amount you have altered is both comfortable and removes the extra fullness.

4 To shorten sleeve length, use your shoulder to elbow measurement to determine whether to adjust either above or below the

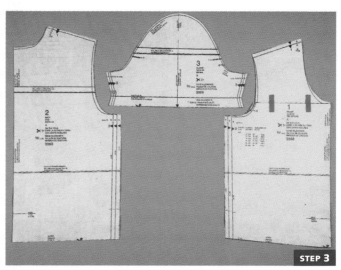

STEP 3

Shortening the pattern between the top and bottom of the armhole allows the upper chest to lie flat.

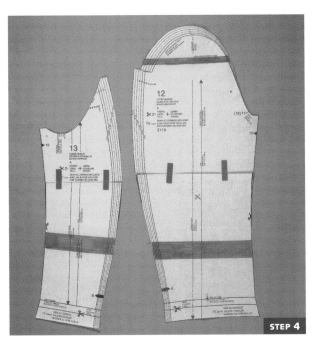

STEP 4

Shorten sleeves both above and below the armhole.

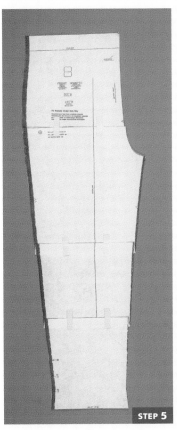

STEP 5

elbow shaping. Draw horizontal lines across the sleeve. Fold out what you don't need, and smooth out jogs at the sides.

5 To shorten skirts and pants without losing the integrity of the style, alter within the body of the garment—never more than 2 in. (5cm) in any one place—rather than just on the bottom edge. Divide the total alteration amount between three different spots: between the waist and the crotch point, the crotch point and the knee, and the knee and the hemline. Draw a horizontal line across the pattern, perpendicular to the grainline. Draw another line 2 in. (5cm) above it. Fold out the amount between the lines and smooth out the jogs at the seams.

If you are petite, spread your alterations among three key spots: between the waist and crotch, the crotch and knee, and the knee to the hem crease.

Broad Back

THE PROBLEM

If the back of your garments feel tight and the back armhole seamlines often rip out, then you're all too familiar with the broad back over-fitting problem. The dilemma with ready-to-wear is difficult: If you buy a garment that fits in front, the back is too tight. Yet, if you buy a garment to fit your back, there's too much fabric in the front.

Few of us have bodies that are divided in perfect halves, so that the front of the body is the same width as the back. This is particularly true when comparing the upper back to the upper front chest. Many people are one size in front and one or two sizes larger across the back. Sometimes age, too, can cause a rounded back and narrowed upper chest. Whatever the case, pattern alterations can dramatically improve your garments.

FAST FIT SOLUTION

On a single-size pattern, add a vertical extension from the shoulder to the hemline. If your pattern is multisize, use a size or two larger when cutting the back (see "Altering Multisize Patterns" on p. 58). To join the seamlines, add an easeline across the back shoulder or, for large alterations, create a dart in the middle of the back shoulder.

STEP-BY-STEP SOLUTION

1 Purchase a pattern that fits your front upper chest and adjust the bust to fit (if necessary) by adding at the side seams.

2 Take a flat pattern measurement across the back pattern piece at the armhole notches, from the side seamline to the center back. Multiply this number by two.

3 Compare the pattern measurement to your own cross back measurement, plus the amount of ease you want. A good rule of thumb is ¾ in. to 1 in. (1.9cm to 2.5cm) of ease across the back. The difference between these numbers is the amount you need to alter your pattern.

4 On the back pattern piece, draw a line from the center of the shoulder to the bottom of the garment, making the line parallel to the grainline. Cut the pattern in two along this line.

5 Halve the alteration amount that you determined in Step 2. Cut a pattern paper extension to this width and insert it, taping it down, between the two halves of back pattern piece. True up the shoulder seam.

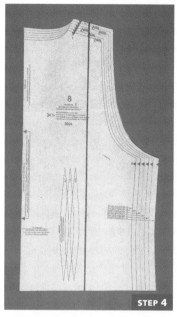

STEP 4

On the back, draw a line from mid-shoulder to hem, parallel to the grainline. The pattern will be cut apart on this line.

Broad Back, *continued*

Adding a small amount of width from top to bottom along the back makes a more comfortable garment for those with a broad back.

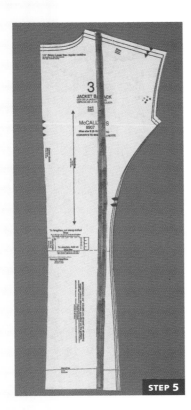

STEP 5

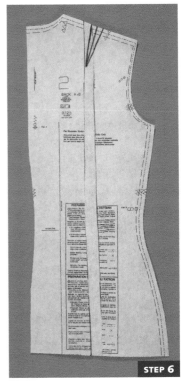

STEP 6

Ease or dart out the excess back shoulder width so that lengths of the front and back shoulder seams match.

6 With this alteration, the back shoulder seamline is now longer than the front. If your pattern alteration is less than ½-in. (1.3cm) wide, an easeline across the back shoulder makes them the same length. If your addition to the back is more than ½ in. (1.3cm), you'll need to create a dart in the middle of the back shoulder. Make the dart as wide as the pattern alteration and 3½ in. (8.1cm) long from the shoulder cutting line. Or you can put only

SIMPLE SIZING

Altering for a broad back is a breeze with a multisize pattern. Simply cut the back one or two sizes larger at the armhole only; the shoulder and neck stay the same size as the front. Cut the front of the sleeve cap to the smaller size, which matches the front pattern piece, and the back of the sleeve cap to the larger size, matching the upper back on your back pattern piece. At the sleeve shoulder placement dot, transition between the two sizes. Now you won't have any difficulty fitting the sleeve into the armhole. Since the back and front shoulder seam lengths no longer match, add a dart or ease the back shoulder to fit.

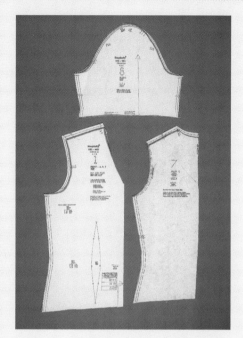

some of the back addition into the dart and ease the remaining ½ in. (1.3cm). The dart can be curved if the upper shoulder is rounded. Then sew the shoulders together with the back closest to the feed dogs. Small darts can be short; wide darts need more length to end smoothly.

Narrow Back

THE PROBLEM

A narrow back is quite common on people with very erect posture. You may have either been born with an upper-torso fitting problem or adopted an erect posture through force of habit. If your garments have vertical wrinkles up and down the back, and horizontal wrinkles between the shoulder blades, it's a good indication that you have a narrow back. From shoulder to waist, your entire back is proportionally smaller than your front.

In this case, both a horizontal and a vertical adjustment are necessary. A typical back alteration is ½ in. (1.3cm), but you may need to fine-tune your alteration. The ideal style for you is one in which the back seams extend from shoulder to hem, so you can take in the seams. Today's Fit patterns by Vogue and Butterick patterns often feature this type of seaming. Whether the entire back—or just the top half—is narrow, the following instructions help create a smooth, wrinkle-free back.

FAST FIT SOLUTION

Reduce the back pattern piece both horizontally and vertically to eliminate all wrinkles. Ease the different-length shoulder seams together. Reduce the sleeve back with a horizontal tuck to match.

STEP-BY-STEP SOLUTION

1 Draw a vertical line, parallel to the grain-line, from mid-shoulder to the waist of the back pattern piece. Draw a second line ½ in. to ¾ in. (1.3cm to 1.9cm) away, toward the armhole.

2 Make a horizontal cut from the waist at the side seam to the vertical lines, so that the pattern is not reduced below the waist. Fold and tape the pattern piece together along the lines, then true up the side seams. This takes care of the vertical wrinkles above the waist.

3 True up the shoulder seam, keeping the neckline size intact. Because the front shoulder is now longer, ease it into the back by sewing with the front shoulder against the feed dogs (see "Joining Uneven Shoulder Seams" on p. 88).

4 To eliminate the horizontal wrinkles, draw a horizontal line across the back pattern piece just above the sleeve notches at the arm-hole. Draw a second line ¼ in. to ½ in. (6mm to 1.3cm) above it, parallel to the first. Fold and tape the pattern piece together along the lines.

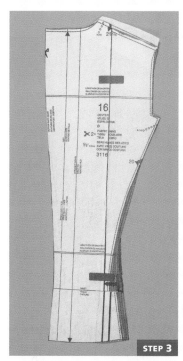

STEP 3

For a better fit on a narrow back, reduce the pattern both horizontally and vertically above the waist. If you need width below the waist, add at the vertical seams.

> **FITTING TIP**
> Before cutting the garment pieces from your fashion fabrics, make a pretest garment. Assess the fit and refine the back pattern piece as necessary.

JOINING UNEVEN SHOULDER SEAMS

Once you've completed the vertical tuck in Step 2 on p. 87, your front shoulder seam may be longer than the back. This is easily remedied if your pattern has a back shoulder dart that can be eliminated. Darts in the shoulder and waistline areas only emphasize the problem of a narrow back and should be ignored. Eliminating the dart will also make the front and back shoulder seams the same size after the vertical tuck.

If the back doesn't have a dart, the front shoulder seam will be longer. In this case, run an easeline ½ in. (1.3cm) from the raw edge on the front shoulder. Press the easing to remove wrinkles without stretching the shoulder area back to the original length. Now sew the back and front shoulders together with right sides facing and the front shoulder closest to the feed dogs. The teeth of the feed dogs will ease in any excess length.

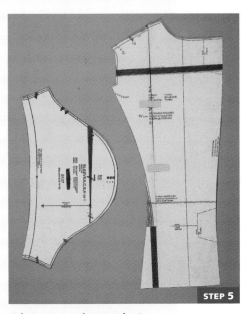

STEP 5

Whatever is taken out horizontally in the back must also be taken out of the sleeve. The reduction should taper to zero by the sleeve front.

5 On the sleeve, draw a horizontal line across the pattern above the notches. Fold out a horizontal tuck in the sleeve back only, tapering to zero by the sleeve front. Smooth out the cutting line on the back of the sleeve cap. Do not change the location of the shoulder placement dot on the sleeve cap; ease the front into the back shoulder when sewing.

Scoliosis

THE PROBLEM

If one side of your back is slightly fuller and higher than the other, it could be an indication of scoliosis, a condition for which you have probably already visited a chiropractor and had diagnosed long before now. As far as garment fit is concerned, scoliosis results in either a diagonal wrinkle across the back that angles toward the full side or a horizontal pleat that angles into the back armhole on the low side. Once the pattern is altered, the wrinkles will disappear and no one will notice that your back is not symmetrical.

FAST FIT SOLUTION

Copy the back bodice and sleeve pattern to create separate pattern pieces for the left and right side. On the full side, lift and spread the back bodice in the shoulder and armhole area to provide more length and width. Lift the sleeve cap back the same amount you raised the bodice back; join the front and back shoulder seams smoothly by running an easeline on the back shoulder.

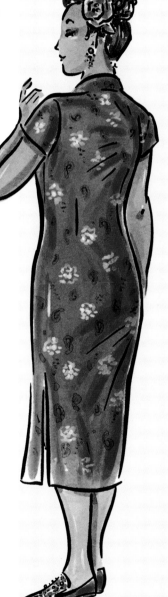

STEP-BY-STEP SOLUTION

1 Trace off the back bodice and sleeve pattern so that you have separate pattern pieces for the left and right sides. Label the pattern pieces, left and right. Determine which side represents the full side of your back.

2 On the full side, draw an L (a backward L if it's the left side or a normal L if it's the right side) from halfway across the shoulder to the bottom of the armhole. Cut the pattern apart on this line.

3 Lift and spread the back bodice about ½ in. (1.3 cm); you may need to increase or decrease this amount after making the first garment. This alteration gives the full side more length and width. Smooth out the shoulder

To eliminate a diagonal wrinkle on the sleeve, raise the sleeve cap by the same amount you raised the bodice back.

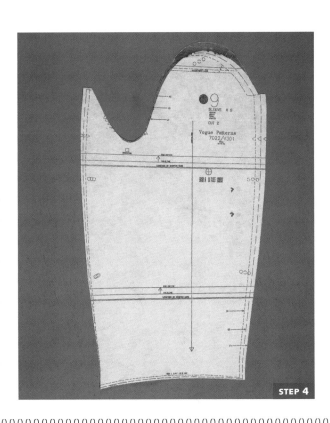

STEP 4

seam by keeping it the same at the neck and letting it rise as it goes toward the armhole. Smooth out side seam under the back armhole.

4 Since the back armhole is now longer, draw a horizontal line across the sleeve cap above the notches. Cut the pattern apart on this line, keeping it intact for ⅜ in. (1cm) near the front notches. Lift the sleeve cap back the same amount you raised the bodice back, letting the addition taper back to zero by the front armhole. The back shoulder seam on the full side is now longer than the front shoulder seam.

5 Run an easeline on the back shoulder seam to make both the front and the back shoulder seams fit together nicely.

Swayback or Down-Sloping Back Waistline

THE PROBLEM

An assortment of fitting difficulties stems from a curvature of the spine, or a swayback. Simply put, there's too much fabric at the back waist: Wrinkles form under the back waistband, pant seats are stretched because the fabric is shifted off-grain, side seams swing forward, and hemlines are longer in back. Even jackets and dresses without waist seams puff out at the back waist.

Raising the center back waistline until the side seams are perpendicular to the floor dramatically improves the appearance of garments, but a change can be made on styles without a waist seam as well. Raising the back waistline also eliminates wrinkles under the back waistband.

FAST FIT SOLUTION

Raise the center back waistline and scoop out the crotch curve slightly to make the crotch more comfortable after the adjustment. The waistband is applied to the new back waistline, eliminating wrinkles under the waistband.

STEP-BY-STEP SOLUTION

1 First, determine the amount you need to raise the back waist. To do this, slip into a finished skirt or pair of pants, stand in front of a mirror, and take a close look at one of the side seams. Lift the garment at center back until your side seam is perfectly straight. Pin the center back in this position. For now, don't worry if the crotch is too tight or the skirt hemline is uneven.

2 Remove the garment and measure the amount that you lifted the center back, usually about ½ in. (1.3cm). (You may have to guess a bit the first time you try this alteration.)

3 On your pattern piece, mark this distance below the waist cutting line at center back. Pin out any darts. Draw a new cutting line from the mark at center back, tapering to the original waist cutting line at the side seam.

4 It is usually necessary to scoop out the crotch curve about ¼ in. (6mm) to make the pants comfortable after the adjustment. If your center back alteration is more than ½ in. (1.3 cm), scoop out ¼ in. (6mm) on the lower crotch curve, and add ¼ in. (6mm) at the back inner leg hook to made the crotch more comfortable.

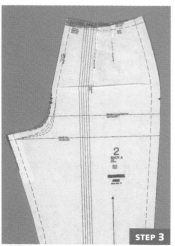

STEP 3

Lift the center back seamline by cutting off at center back and tapering to zero by the side seam.

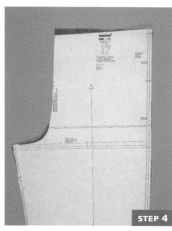

STEP 4

An alteration at center back waistline often requires more room in the crotch. Scoop out the lower crotch curve slightly to make pants more comfortable.

BACK GAPOSIS

For a coat, dress, or jacket without a waist seam, gaposis (puffing out) at center back can be remedied. Fold out no more than ½ in. (1.3cm) horizontally at center back near the waistline. After cutting out the garment pieces, clip ⅜ in. (1cm) into the seam allowances five times in the area between 2½ in. (6.4cm) above and below the waist. Now, when you join the front and back, you can stretch the back seam allowance. On a two-piece back, both pieces must be adjusted with clips at the side back seamlines where they join the side fronts.

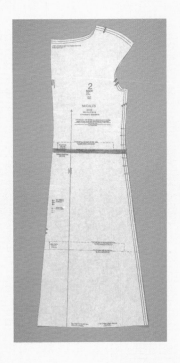

5 If the pattern has side back seams, as on a gored skirt, taper the new back waistband cutting line gradually across the back and side back pattern pieces. If the side back pattern piece doesn't have a side seam, mark one on the pattern and taper the new waist cutting line to that mark.

6 Cut the garment pieces from the fabric, following the new "dipped" line at the back waistline. The waistband is then applied to these curved pieces; but the curve is so gradual, you won't notice it after sewing. Your side seam will be perpendicular to the floor, without any wrinkles under the back waistband.

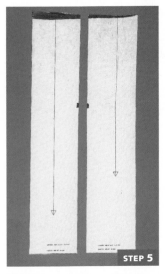

STEP 5

If you are using two pieces, cut more off the center piece, tapering across to zero by the side seam.

Round Upper Back

THE PROBLEM

Our upper back tends to round as we age, preventing the back neckline from seating properly on our neck. The back's roundness pulls the back neckline down, causing it to ride too low. As a result, the collar sticks out in center back and even prevents the front from hanging properly. In addition, the rounded back also steals from the lower back, so the back of the jacket gets shorter and winds up sticking out.

Men come in all shapes and sizes, yet their suit jackets always fit smoothly across the entire back. The key to such good fit is a seam at center back that can be taken in or let out to mimic the body's shape. Instead of cutting the center back on the fold, a center back seam provides more flexibility. Patterns that include a center back seam are always going to give you a better fit, but you can also add a center back seam where the pattern tells you to cut on fold. This technique is especially good if you have a curved back or a protruding backside. The following simple change yields great results; the sleeve and collar pattern pieces don't even need to be touched.

FAST FIT SOLUTION

Start with a wider center back seam allowance and vary the width to release or take in fabric. Add length between the shoulder and the bottom of the armhole. In cases when you prefer not to have a center back seam, another method can also give you the length you need (see "Altering without a Center Back Seam" on the facing page).

STEP-BY-STEP SOLUTION

1 To add a center back seam where the pattern says to cut on fold, tape a pattern paper extension to the cut-on-fold line to make a center back seam allowance. Try a center back seam allowance width of 1½ in. (3.8cm) so that you have fabric to play with.

2 Determine how much length to add. To do this, either make a pretest or try on something collarless from your wardrobe that should ride at the back of the neck on the natural neckline, such as a collarless jacket or blouse. Put on a small necklace. The clasp on the back of the necklace indicates the ideal location of the neckline on the jacket. If you have a rounded back, your neckline may be anywhere from ½ in. to 1½ in. (1.3cm to 3.8cm) down from the clasp of the necklace. Measure this amount and use it as an alteration amount for rounded back.

3 On the back pattern piece in the top third of the armhole, draw a horizontal line across the pattern from center back to the bottom of the armhole. Cut through the line from center back to within ⅜ in. (1cm) of the armhole cutting line. A small bit of pattern paper at the armhole now holds the upper back to the lower part of the pattern piece.

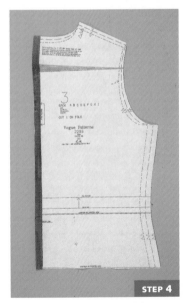

STEP 4

A rounded back needs extra length, which is added in the upper third of the bodice above the armhole. Adding a seam allowance rather than cutting on the fold allows the upper back seam to curve in.

Suppose you are making a blouse and don't want a seam in the center back? For the same effect, draw a horizontal line perpendicular to the grainline across the back, in the upper third of the back armhole. Draw another line perpendicular to the first, starting at mid-shoulder down to the first line. Cut the pattern apart along these lines. Move up the upper back section and tape it in place. Smooth out the shoulder cutting line by keeping the original neck point and the shoulder armhole point the same.

4 Lift the upper back the amount you need, then taper the spread to nothing at the armhole. Tape a piece of pattern paper under the spread and smooth the center back cutting line between the upper and lower section of the back bodice. The center back seam now slants in slightly near the neck, which works because you're using a seam at center back rather than cutting the pattern piece on the fold. The curved seam mimics your back curve.

5 If the pattern you are altering has a two-piece back, alter the center back piece the entire amount of the alteration (that is, the amount you want to lift the upper back), tapering slightly as you go toward the side back seam. Spread the side back a smaller amount, corresponding to the center back taper. The side back should taper to zero by the armhole seamline.

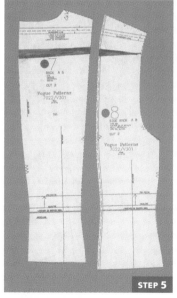

STEP 5

When the back has two pattern pieces, such as back and side back, make the whole adjustment on the center back piece. The side back adjustment tapers to zero by the armhole.

Full Back High Hip

THE PROBLEM

If you have a high hip in back, you may have caught a glimpse of yourself in a three-way mirror sometime and noticed that your clothes get hung up on the high hip in back. If this is the case, you need to choose patterns with a side back seam to get more fabric over the back high hip so the garment can slide off without drawing attention to the fitting problem. An added bonus: Your skirts won't be shorter in the back ever again. A pattern without princess seams in back is a problem for this figure, because you are trying to put a flat piece of fabric over a highly curved part of the body. No matter how much fabric you have, it's still going to get caught up on the back high hip. On the other hand, garments with princess seams in back provide two seams to contour, so the fabric can be shaped to fit smoothly over the hip.

If you have this type of figure and are looking for jacket and coat patterns, look for patterns with princess seams in back, such as Vogue 7022 or Vogue 7183. At the very least, find patterns with a center back seam that can be curved. Cut extra-wide seam allowances on the princess seams in back, 1 in. (2.5cm) beyond the cutting line. This will give you some leeway for fitting over the protruding back high hip. If you don't want seams in a blouse, you'll need to add some back darts to provide shaping.

FAST FIT SOLUTION

To prevent jackets, vests, and blouses from getting hung up on a full back high hip, princess seams need to be let out to fit smoothly over the high hip and contour in to the waist. Allow for wider seam allowances when cutting and enlist a friend to help you do the fitting.

STEP-BY-STEP SOLUTION

1 From scrap fabric, cut only the front and back pieces of a jacket. Machine-baste the jacket together on its actual seamlines.

2 Enlist the help of a friend. Try on the jacket inside out. Ask your friend to release the back princess seams with a seam ripper to about 2 in. (5cm) above the waist and to repin them so there is enough fabric to go over the high hip smoothly.

3 Transfer the new seamlines to the pattern.

4 A protruding back high hip often goes with a narrow and short upper back. While your friend is repinning the back seams below the waist, also ask her to pin out any unnecessary fabric in the seams above the waist. Transfer any seam changes to the pattern.

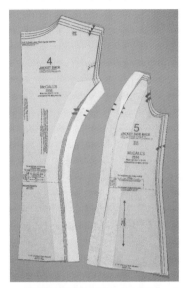

Cutting extra-wide seam allowances on the side back seams allow you to fit over the full high hip smoothly by letting out the seam.

The Shoulders

Uneven Shoulders

THE PROBLEM

If it were possible to study your shoulders from the back, it would be easy to see if they were uneven. But because this isn't a typical point of view, your garments may be giving off signals that are easier to recognize. Shoulders that are not level result in a diagonal wrinkle going from the higher shoulder across the front or back of the garment. Other indications of uneven shoulders include a neckline that gapes on one side and a collar that looks off-center.

Many people weren't born with uneven shoulders but acquired them after a lifetime of carrying babies, purses, or other heavy objects on one side of their body. The good news is that, with a little alteration, this problem is easily solved. Although they might seem complicated, the alterations are relatively simple, and the results are spectacular. A pretest garment is also helpful in this case, to reveal if the seam allowances on one shoulder are deeper than on the other (see "Pretesting a Pattern" on p. 46).

FAST FIT SOLUTION

Alterations are needed on several pattern pieces: the bodice front, bodice back, facings, and collar. On your low shoulder side, lower the entire shoulder seamline and the underarm seamline on the bodice front and back. Adjust the collar and facings to match the new neckline.

STEP-BY-STEP SOLUTION

1 Cut out the garment pieces with 1-in.
(2.5cm) seam allowances on the shoulder
seams. Baste the shoulder and side seams together, slip on the garment, and pin the front
or back opening closed. Pin a deeper seam allowance on the low shoulder to reflect your
shape. Remove the garment and mark the new
seamline on the garment and the pattern
pieces.

2 Measure the distance between the old and
new shoulder seamlines.

3 The amount that you lowered the seamline
at the low shoulder must also be taken
away at the underarm on the front and back
garment pieces, so that the size of the armhole
remains the same. Starting at the side seam,
lower the armhole cutting line the same
amount that you lowered the shoulder. Taper
the new line back to the original at the lower
armhole notches. No alterations are needed
on the sleeve.

4 Since the front and back facings also have
shoulder seams, a small alteration is made
on the shoulder seam of the facing on the low
side. Because the low shoulder alteration usually tapers to zero by the neckline, the facing
seam allowance deepens just a bit near the
outer edge, tapering back to the original at the
neckline. The easiest technique is to sew the
seam allowance deeper on the low side.

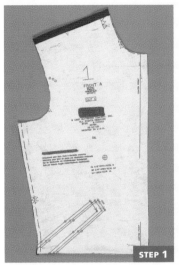

STEP 1

Cut out the bodice front
and back with wider seam
allowances, so seams can
be shaped to fit the slope
of your shoulders.

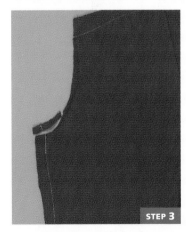

STEP 3

To keep the armhole the same
size, lower the underarm by
the same amount you lowered
the shoulder.

5 Any collar that extends onto the shoulder must be altered at the outside edge, on the low shoulder side only. It is no longer possible to cut the collar piece on a fold. (Neckbands and stand-up collars are not altered, since the neckline remains the same.) Trace the half-collar pattern piece onto pattern paper to make a full collar and transfer the shoulder markings. On the low shoulder side of the collar, take out the same amount that you lowered the shoulder seam, but double the amount that you took away from the bodice shoulder seamline to compensate for front and back alterations. For example, if you lowered a shoulder by ¼ in. (6mm), then take ½ in. (1.3cm) out of the collar on the low side. Fold this out of the collar, on the outside edge only, at the shoulder seamline placement dot on the low shoulder side. Smooth out the cutting line.

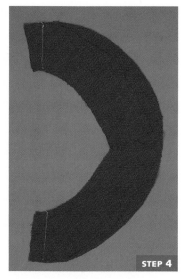

STEP 4

On the low side, the facing seam allowance is sewn deeper on the outside edge.

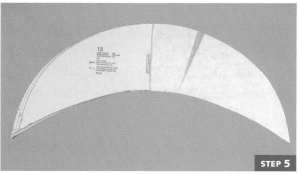

STEP 5

Cut the collar apart on the low shoulder side, leaving it intact at the neck edge. Then overlap the cut edge to reduce the collar, on the outside edge only, by the same amount that was taken out of the shoulder.

Fleshy Shoulders

THE PROBLEM

If your shoulders are full right at the base of the neck, vertical wrinkles will point to the shoulder near the neck in front, and wrinkles may form right under the collar in back. You may have this problem on only one side if you tend to favor a particular side while lifting heavy objects. The key here is to add extra fabric in the shoulder seam near the neck, allowing the garment to release and relax over the shoulder's fullness. Once the pattern is altered, these wrinkles will disappear, giving a clean, flat fit in the upper chest.

FAST FIT SOLUTION

Determine where the addition needs to be made: back shoulders only, both front and back bodice pieces, or only on one shoulder. Make the addition; then adjust the facings by the same amount. Lengthen the collar by the same amount at the approximate location of the shoulder seam addition.

STEP-BY-STEP SOLUTION

1 If wrinkles form in the back only, right under the collar seam, an addition is needed on the back shoulder only. To determine the exact amount to add, you'll need to pretest a pattern. Begin by adding ¼ in. (6mm) to the back shoulder near the neck. Taper the addition to the original cutting line by the armhole.

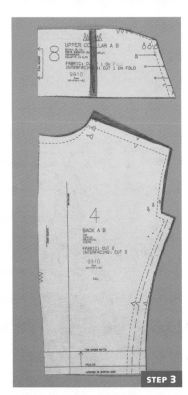

Add to the back shoulder, tapering to zero by the armhole. An identical alteration must be made on the back facing and the collar.

2 Make an identical alteration on the back facing.

3 Because the neckline is now larger, your collar must be lengthened to accommodate the larger neckline. Cut the collar apart at the approximate location of the shoulder seam. Add ¼ in. (6mm) to the collar pattern.

4 If a vertical wrinkle points to the bottom of the neckline where it joins the shoulder in front, both front and back bodice pieces need to be increased at the neckline. To determine exact amounts, you will need to release the shoulder seam until the vertical wrinkle disappears. On the shoulder seam, take out the stitches for about 3 in. (7.6cm) near the neck, leaving the shoulder seam intact as it nears the armhole. Let the bodice relax. The seam will separate and whatever the distance is between the seamlines is the total alteration. Divide this in two and add half to the front and half to the back. For example, if the neckline splits apart ½ in. (1.3cm), a ¼-in. (6mm) addition is needed on the front and the back, tapering to zero by the armhole. This will increase the size of the neckline by ½ in. (1.3cm) on each side.

5 Facings must be adjusted identically. If the garment has a collar, split and spread the collar pattern at the shoulder seam location and add the same amount as the front and back shoulder additions.

6 Some people need this alteration on one side only; this is
indicated by a vertical wrinkle on
just one side. In this case, the
shoulder seams are sewn differently on the left and right sides.
And there's no need to cut left and
right sides singly. Instead, simply
cut wider seam allowances on the
shoulders so that one side can be
let out without the seam allowance
getting too skimpy.

7 The collar cannot be cut on
the fold, since more length on
the collar is needed on one side
only. Simply cut a mirror image of
the collar pattern piece. Tape the
collar pieces together at center
back. Lengthen the collar piece on
the side where the addition to the
shoulder seam was made.

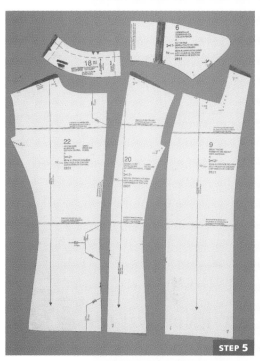

STEP 5

Adjustments made on the
shoulder seams near the neck
affect both facings and collars.
Identical alterations must
be made on these pieces.

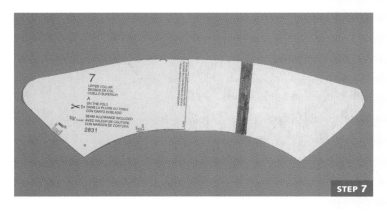

STEP 7

Collar adjustments
must be made on
only one side when
the shoulder seam
is let out near the
neckline. Make
a template of the
collar and adjust
the affected side.

IDENTIFYING SHOULDER PROBLEMS

Do you find that many of your garments have tight armholes? Or are there diagonal wrinkles across the bodice? How about a baggy bodice? The shape of your shoulders is likely the root of all these problems. But before making any alterations, you need to know what shape your shoulders are. For example, the problem could be a result of sloping shoulders; square shoulders; or high, low, or uneven shoulders.

If you're unhappy with the way your garments fit in the upper chest area, read the descriptions for all of the problems relating to the shoulders or experiment with some alterations if you think you know the problem. Once you know the shape of your shoulders and the alteration amounts, you can make the right adjustments on every pattern.

Make a Pretest Garment

The best starting point is to make a simple pretest garment. This helps you identify your figure problem and determine the amount and location of the alteration.

1 Cut the bodice front and back garment pieces from a fabric scrap, using 1½-in. (3.8cm) seam allowances at the shoulders. Mark the center front and back on the garment pieces. Also mark the seamlines.

2 Staystitch or stay-tape the neckline seam. Clip the seam allowance to the staystitching. Baste the side seams together in a contrasting thread color.

Looking in the mirror can provide a good indication of shoulder fitting problems, but the most reliable information comes from making a pretest garment. By pinning the shoulder seam to fit your shape, you'll find out what alterations need to be made.

STEP 3

This pretest garment is ready to try on, with 1½-in. (3.8cm) wide seam allowances, a stay-taped neckline seam, a clipped neck curve, and clearly marked seamlines.

3 Turn the pretest garment right side out and try on the bodice. (If you try on the garment wrong side out, you may end up altering the wrong side.) Pin the front or back opening closed. With wrong sides together, pin the shoulder seams together along the seamline, with the seam allowances sticking out of the garment. Adjust the pins so that the bodice hangs perfectly straight and the dart points and waistline sit in the correct locations. Check that the shoulder seam isn't too far to the front or back; you shouldn't be able to see a correctly positioned shoulder seam when viewing the garment at eye level.

4 Take off the bodice without removing the pins in the shoulders. The seam allowance depths indicate the shoulder problem and tell you the size of the adjustment that you need to make.

- A sloping shoulder has a deeper seam allowance near the armhole.

- Square shoulders have smaller seam allowances near the armhole.

- A low shoulder has a deeper seam allowance from the armhole to the neckline.

- A high shoulder has a narrower seam allowance near the armhole.

- Fleshy shoulders have a narrower seam allowance near the neck.

Keep in mind that both shoulders may not be the same. Or you might have a combination low and sloping shoulder, which is indicated by a narrower seam allowance near the neck and a wider seam allowance closer to the armhole.

The pins in this shoulder seam have been placed so that the shape of the garment mimics the shoulder shape.

Look closely at the pins, which will indicate the alteration: sloping shoulders have deeper seams near the armhole, and square shoulders have smaller seams near the armhole.

Narrow Shoulders

THE PROBLEM

If your garments sometimes look too big, narrow shoulders could be the problem. Narrow shoulders cause shoulder seams to sit improperly—usually falling off the shoulder, giving the appearance of an off-shoulder garment even when that's not the intended style. The shoulder seam on set-in sleeves will not be positioned at the joint of the shoulder and the arm; as a result, the garment is uncomfortable, restricts movement, and is extremely unflattering. After experimenting with many alteration techniques, I have settled on the one given here. It does not affect either the size or the shape of the armhole, making sleeve changes unnecessary.

FAST FIT SOLUTION

Mark a new cutting line on the shoulder. Make a copy of the upper halves of the front and back bodices to determine the right amount to raise the armhole. Run an easeline on the back shoulder to make the front and back shoulder lengths match. No sleeve adjustment is required.

STEP-BY-STEP SOLUTION

1 Make a copy of your front and back bodices from the bustline up—about 2 in. (5cm) down from the bottom of the armhole—by tracing the pattern onto a piece of paper.

2 Cut out the garment everywhere except the front and back armholes. Tape some additional paper in the armhole of the original pattern.

3 On your original pattern piece, make a mark on the shoulder where you would like the new cutting line to be. You can determine this either by looking in the mirror or by comparing your shoulder length measurement to the shoulder length on the pattern, which is measured from the natural neckline to one armhole seam.

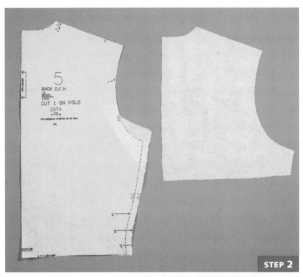

STEP 2

Make a template of the upper front and back bodices. Note that extra paper has been added at the armhole of the original pattern piece.

4 Superimpose your pattern copy onto the pattern original, positioning the top of the armhole in line with the new mark on the shoulder seam indicating the adjusted cutting line.

5 Using your new shoulder seam and armhole location as a pivot point, turn the paper copy out so that it aligns with the side seam. The bottom of the armhole will be raised slightly from the original at the side seam. (This is not a problem because you will be doing the same thing on the back.) Trace the new armhole only. The rest of the pattern will be cut in its original position.

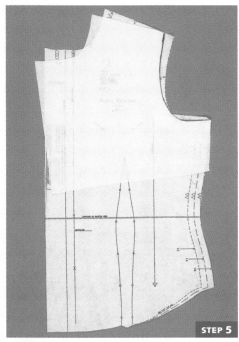

STEP 5

Overlay the template onto the pattern, moving in the shoulder to the desired location. Use the new armhole location on the shoulder as a pivot point to determine the new cutting line.

6 Cut a new armhole using your traced line as a pattern. Only the armhole has changed, effectively shortening the length of the shoulder seam.

7 If you have narrow shoulders but are broad in back, you may want to reduce the shoulder width on the front only. In this case, you will need to raise the back armhole ¼ in. (6mm) on the bodice so that the length of the side seams will match.

8 To make the front and back shoulders match in length, run an easeline on the back shoulder if the difference between front and back shoulders is less than ½ in. (1.3cm); if it is more, insert a small dart midway across the back shoulder seam.

For a combination narrow shoulders/broad back, reduce the width of the front shoulder. The only alteration needed on the back bodice is to raise the underarm by ¼ in. (6mm) so that the lengths of the side seams match.

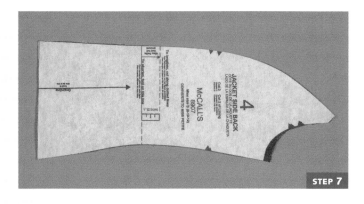

STEP 7

Sloping Shoulders

THE PROBLEM

A dead giveaway for sloping shoulders is the appearance of diagonal wrinkles near the armholes. Shoulder pads might take care of the problem, but most women don't want to wear shoulder pads with every garment. And if your shoulders slope quite a bit, the shoulder pads would have to be relatively thick and thus bulky.

To determine if sloping shoulders are the culprit, try the pinch test: Put on a blouse and use your fingers to pinch up the bodice on the shoulder, near the sleeve joint. If the wrinkles disappear, you've got sloping shoulders. A pretest garment is also helpful for detecting this problem—you'll find that the seam allowances on sloping shoulders are deeper at the armhole and angle to the standard width at the neckline.

Also, both shoulders may not slope the same amount, which is also uncovered in a pretest. If they are very similar, make the shoulders the same on both sides. If one slopes and the other doesn't, you'll need to cut the pattern pieces singly in the armhole and shoulder area.

Sloping Shoulders, *continued*

The pinch test is a great indicator that sloping shoulders are the problem: If the wrinkles disappear when fabric is pinched up at the shoulder, it's a sure sign of sloping shoulders.

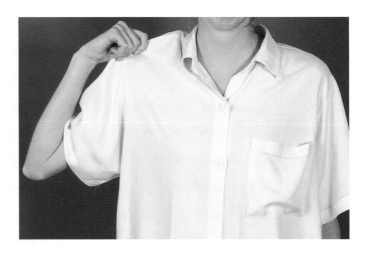

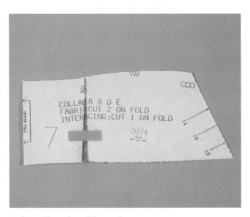

When the shoulders slope, the shoulder seam is taken in near the armhole. Consequently, the collar must also be reduced on the outside edge of the neck, tapering to zero by the neckline.

FAST FIT SOLUTION

Make a pretest garment and determine the slope of your shoulders by pinning the seam allowances to follow their shape. The same amount that you alter the shoulder seamline must also be taken away at the underarm on both the front and back pattern pieces.

STEP-BY-STEP SOLUTION

1 Cut out the garment pieces with 1-in. (2.5cm) seam allowances. Baste the shoulder and side seams together.

2 Slip on the garment right side out and pin the front or back opening closed. Pin deeper seam allowances that follow the shape of your shoulders. The seam allowances will be deeper at the end of the shoulder seam nearest the armhole and taper to the original cutting line at the neck.

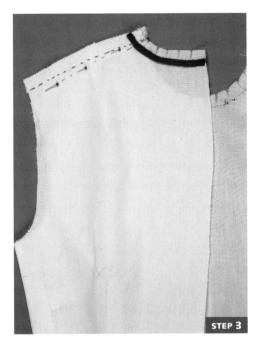

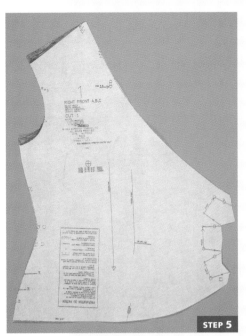

Deeper seam allowances on the shoulder seam near the armhole indicate a sloping shoulder.

Whatever amount you lowered the shoulder must also be lowered at the bottom of the armhole. Finish the alteration by the armhole notches.

3 Remove the garment. Mark the new seamline on the garment pieces.

4 Measure the distance between the old and new shoulder seamlines. The amount that you lower the shoulder at the armhole seamline must also be taken away at the underarm on the front and back garment pieces.

5 Starting at the side seam, lower the armhole cutting line the same amount that you lowered the shoulder. Taper the new cutting line back to the original at the lower armhole notches. Identical alterations should be made on both front and back. No alterations are necessary on the sleeve.

Square Shoulders

THE PROBLEM

Square shoulders have less of a downward angle than usual. As a result, your garments are likely to have a horizontal wrinkle from shoulder to shoulder, directly under the neck. On a pretest garment, if your shoulder seam allowances are narrow at the armhole and angle back to the original seamline at the neck, then it's a good indication that you have square shoulders.

FAST FIT SOLUTION

Make a pretest garment to determine the exact amount of the alteration. Add to the shoulder seamline at the armhole on the front and back bodice; then raise the bottom of the armhole the same amount. No adjustment is required for the sleeve or for facings and collars, unless they are very wide.

STEP-BY-STEP SOLUTION

1 Make a quick pretest garment with 1-in. (2.5cm) basted seam allowances. Try on the pretest with the shoulder seams open. Pin the seam allowance depth at the shoulder seams to fit your body. The seam allowance will be narrower at the armhole than at the neck.

2 Measure the width of the seam allowance near the armhole; this is your alteration amount for the pattern pieces. If measurements are almost the same on both sides, make the same alteration on both shoulders.

FITTING TIP

If you have square shoulders, you might want to avoid boat necklines. They draw attention to the problem.

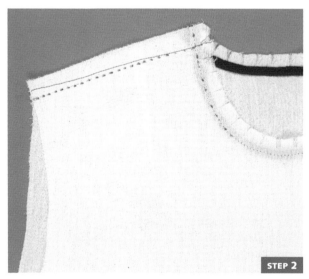

STEP 2

Let out the shoulder seam near the armhole to allow for a square shoulder.

The underarm must be raised by the same amount that was added to the shoulder. No alteration is needed on the sleeve.

3 On front and back bodice pieces, tape extra paper under the shoulder seams. Add height to the shoulder near the armhole, tapering back to the original cutting line by the neckline.

4 To return the armhole to its original size, raise the bottom of the armhole the same amount you raised the shoulder.

5 If one shoulder is more square than the other and you have one pattern piece for the bodice front, you'll need to make a copy to alter the high shoulder side only. Trace the unaltered pattern onto another piece of pattern paper. Label one piece "left front" and the other "right front." Cross off the "Cut 2" instruction on the original pattern piece, change it to "Cut 1," and write it on the traced front.

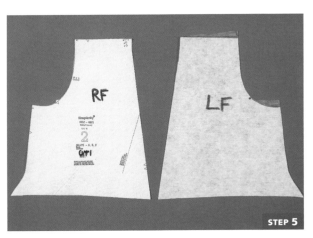

If only one shoulder is square, make a template of the bodice so you can alter only the high side.

SLEEVE SWAP

If you have a favorite sleeve style, why not use it on different garments? Pattern pieces for same-style sleeves are often interchangeable if they're the same size and, preferably, from the same pattern company. If you find a sleeve that suits you better than the one that came with your pattern, make sure that the original and the substitute are the same pattern size. It's equally important that the sleeve styles match in shoulder style. In other words, an off-shoulder sleeve is too flat for a garment that's been designed for set-in sleeves.

Before making the switch, measure the bodice armhole and the sleeve armhole at the seamline to make sure they will fit together. If the sleeve is smaller than the armhole or if the sleeve is more than 2 in. (5cm) bigger than the armhole, it won't work.

6 If your back pattern piece tells you to cut on the fold, trace the shape onto pattern paper. Tape it to the center back foldline of the original back pattern piece. Alter the high shoulder side. Cut the left and right fronts and the back pattern piece from a single layer of fabric.

SHOULDERS AND SLEEVE STYLES

There are a variety of sleeve styles to choose from; but before you decide on one, consider your shoulder and arm shaping. Some sleeve styles are more flattering than others, and the kind of seams that are used can make it easier—or harder—to adjust pattern pieces to fit your own shoulder and arm shaping. The following is a guide to the most appropriate styles and the easiest shapes to alter.

Set-In Sleeves

Set-in sleeves join the bodice at the natural joint of the body where the arm meets the shoulder. They are the top choice for flattering shoulder fit. This style makes a woman look smaller, because you get a closer fit across the upper chest and under the armholes. Set-in sleeves are sometimes avoided because they require a bit more time and sewing expertise than other types

There are a variety of sleeve styles, but some styles address fitting problems better than others. Once you find a style that's right for you, almost any pattern can be altered to include your favorite sleeve.

Set-in sleeves

Dolman sleeves

Drop shoulders

Raglan sleeves

Set in sleeves, as shown on this blouse, are the most flattering sleeve style.

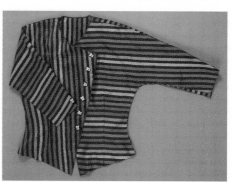

Dolman sleeves give a nice smooth line and are forgiving on anyone with shoulder problems. Try to avoid an especially low curve in the underarm area.

of sleeves, but they are worth the extra effort when you see the flattering results in the mirror.

Dolman Sleeves

A dolman sleeve incorporates the bodice and the sleeve into one piece, making it the easiest sleeve style of all to construct. Dolman sleeves create a smooth line over the upper chest. The dolman sleeve and underarm seam can always be raised to suit your tastes. You can easily adjust the pattern pieces to fit by increasing or decreasing the width of the seam allowances. This is an excellent style for someone with any kind of shoulder problem. If you have square shoulders, you'll need to cut wider seam allowances to let out the shoulders.

ALTERING THE DOLMAN SLEEVE

If you would like to wear dolman sleeves but find that the curve underarm is too low for you, it can be raised as you cut out. The goal is to keep the bust and sleeve circumference the same, but lift the curve up into

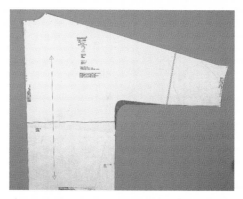

If a dolman sleeve seems too deep for you, don't skip it altogether—simply raise the underarm curve as you cut out.

the sleeve. Start by continuing the side seam up 1 in. to 2 in. (2.5cm to 5cm) into the sleeve, then curve back out into the sleeve. Curved seams at the underarm must be clipped or serged close to lie flat. If you need to get rid of more fabric, you can do it in the sewing; but a conservative approach is better to start with.

Raglan sleeves give an excellent fit if you have shoulder problems, a hollow upper chest, or even a rounded back. Seams can be tapered in and out to mold better to the body.

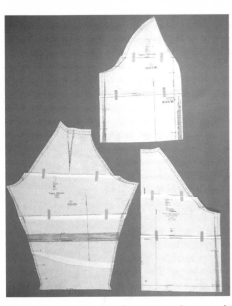

Downsize a raglan by shortening above and below the armhole on both the sleeve and the body of the garment.

Raglan Sleeves

A raglan sleeve incorporates part of the bodice into the sleeve, forming a diagonal line from the neckline to the underarm. Raglan sleeves rank high for fit and altering ease, thanks to the diagonal seams and the shoulder dart in the sleeve. You can easily adjust the pattern pieces by increasing or decreasing the width of the shoulder dart or seam on a raglan. Raglan sleeves are easy to put in because the sleeve does not need to be eased to the bodice and the seams are relatively straight compared to the round seam of a set-in sleeve. The seam that joins the raglan sleeve to the bodice can also be taken in for a narrow front chest or back or can be let out for a broad upper chest or back.

DOWNSIZING THE RAGLAN AND DOLMAN SLEEVE

Both the dolman and the raglan sleeve can be overpowering on someone small, but there's no need to eliminate them from the styles you can wear. To downsize the sleeve, outline the smallest size on the pattern pieces, transitioning to larger sizes smoothly if you need it below the armhole. Shorten the body of the garment and the sleeves above the notches in the armhole, because they are usually too long. If you have narrow shoulders, shorten the dart on the top of the sleeve. Smooth out all of the cutting lines using a curved ruler.

Drop Shoulders

Drop shoulders are created by a wider bodice that hangs off the shoulder onto the arm 1 in. to 2 in. (2.5cm to 5cm) and a flattened sleeve cap that's joined in a seam. Drop shoulders should be used with caution. In general, they aren't flattering unless they're loose fitting and made from a fabric that has lots of drape. A blouse works in this shape, but a coat or a jacket ends up looking baggy. The drop style should particularly be avoided if you have shoulder problems: It draws attention to sloping shoulders, and broad shoulders look even wider. And a narrow-shouldered woman looks as if she raided her big sister's closet. Drop shoulders are definitely not my favorite.

Sometimes you simply can't resist a pattern with drop styling, knowing in your heart that it will hang too far off the shoulder and the armhole will be too deep. So when you open up the pattern and see that your suspicions were well founded, here are some alterations you can make before you cut.

Shorten the bodice front and back 1 in. to 2 in. (2.5cm to 5cm). Smooth out the jogs in the armhole, then bring the top of the armhole on the front and back in 1 in. (2.5cm). The big surprise is that nothing needs to be done with the sleeve! Because you shortened the bodice you need to shorten the sleeve cap the same amount, but because you brought in the shoulder, the cap needs to be raised and the alterations cancel out each other. If possible, always do a quickie pretest for an off-shoulder style, because it still may not be worth making.

Drop shoulders can be unflattering, unless you're using very drapey fabric.

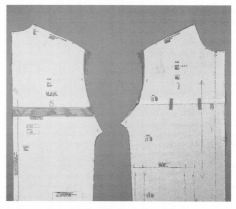

To improve the fit of drop shoulders, shorten between the top and bottom of the armhole and bring in the shoulder. No alteration is needed on the sleeve.

The Sleeves

Large Upper Arms

THE PROBLEM

When it comes to garment fit, it's easy to tell if you have large arms—you simply can't fit your arm into the sleeve on many garments. Even if your arm does fit, often there is not enough movement ease, making the sleeve uncomfortable and restricting your movement.

The first step is determining where, exactly, your sleeve gets hung up: the forearm, the upper arm, the cap, or all three places (see "Determining Sleeve Size" on p. 133). Start the improvement process by making sure that you are altering the right spot. To allow enough room for free, unrestricted movement, you'll need to take specific arm measurements with your arm bent.

FAST FIT SOLUTION

Pinpoint the problem area and add the necessary amount, including ease, to the sleeve pattern piece. If your pattern is multisize, cut the sleeve larger than the rest of the garment. If not, split and spread the sleeve pattern piece from cap to hem, easing the sleeve all the way around to fit the existing armhole.

STEP-BY-STEP SOLUTION

Adding Less Than ¾ in. (1.9cm)

1 Highlight the sleeve size you are using on the pattern. Make any necessary alterations in length. Mark the vertical seam allowances on the sleeve pieces so you won't be tempted to include them in your measurements.

2 Measure across the sleeve pattern between the seam allowances at the three locations that correspond to your arm measurements: right under the armhole; 3 in. (7.6cm) below the armhole; and on the forearm, about 10 in. (25.4cm) below the armhole. If you have long or short arms, alter the sleeve length before measuring. On a two-piece sleeve, measure both parts in all three locations, first on the under sleeve and then the upper sleeve in the same locations. Try to keep your measurements perpendicular to the grainline.

3 Compare your body measurements plus ease to the pattern measurements and assess the pattern design ease. If the pattern is multi-size, you can simply cut the sleeve a size or two larger than the rest of the garment. Then, instead of running an easeline just between the notches on the sleeve cap, run the easeline all around the sleeve to fit into the armhole. You can also use

FITTING FACT

If you have a large upper arm, you'll draw attention to it if you fit the forearm too close.

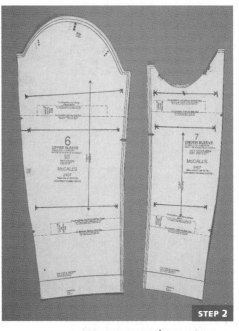

STEP 2

Measure your sleeve pieces between seamlines in three locations: right under the armhole, 3 in. (7.6cm) lower, and across the forearm.

Large Upper Arms, *continued*

Multisize patterns make it easy to cut a size or two larger sleeve if your arms are large. Fit into the armhole by running ease all around the sleeve.

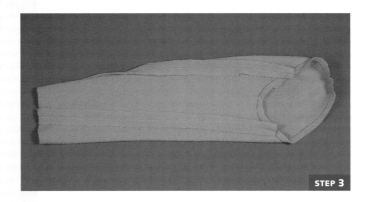

STEP 3

FITTING TIP
Pretest just the sleeve pattern piece in scrap fabric to ensure that there is enough room around the upper arm and sufficient height in the cap. Look for horizontal wrinkles across the cap (cap is not wide enough) and vertical wrinkles (cap is too short).

a larger size in the upper arm and taper in to a smaller size for the forearm. If you need ¾ in. (1.9cm) or less in arm girth and your fullness is high in the upper arm, split and spread the sleeve pattern piece from cap to hem, making the spread narrower near the hem.

4 To split and spread the sleeve, cut the sleeve in half vertically. Spread it as necessary, to a maximum of ¾ in. (1.9cm), and tape

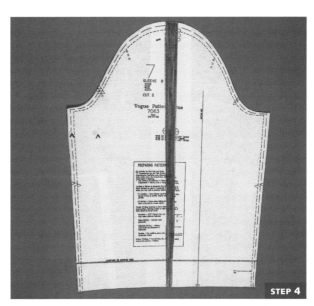

STEP 4

If you need only a slightly larger sleeve and your fullness is in the cap area, split and spread the cap, tapering at the bottom of the sleeve if you don't need extra in the forearm.

in a pattern paper extension to hold the pieces together. If you need less in the forearm, taper the spread as it goes down the sleeve.

5 After cutting out the garment pieces and sewing the underarm seam, sew two ease-lines ½ in. (1.3cm) from the cut edge of the entire sleeve, not just on the cap between the front and back notches. Press and shape the sleeve ease over a tailor's ham before inserting it into the garment armhole.

Adding More Than ¾ in. (1.9cm)

When the pattern is not multisized or you need to add more than ¾ in. (1.9cm) to the largest size, use the following technique. This alteration adds only a small amount at the sleeve cap seamline so you will not have difficulty easing in a larger sleeve.

1 Draw a line vertically on the sleeve pattern from the dot on the cap, keeping the ruler parallel with the grainline, to the bottom of the sleeve.

2 Draw a second line horizontally across the pattern at the bottom of the cap, perpendicular to the grainline.

3 Slide a piece of paper under the pattern. Cut the pattern apart along the lines, leaving the pattern intact for ⅝ in. (1.5cm) at all edges.

4 From the sides of the sleeve pattern, pull the pattern apart to create a gap that equals

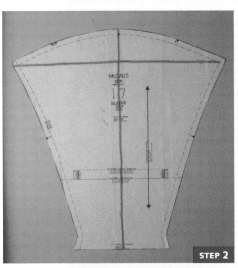

STEP 2

Draw a vertical line from shoulder dot to sleeve bottom. Draw a horizontal line across the sleeve at the bottom of the cap.

the amount you want to add to the sleeve. You will notice that the pattern overlaps a bit horizontally as the pattern spreads.

5 Tape the expanded sleeve pattern onto the paper. To the sleeve cap and bottom of the sleeve, add the amount of the horizontal overlap in the middle, which will be about ½ in. (1.3cm) at the top of the cap and ½ in. (1.3cm) at the bottom of the sleeve. Taper off the addition on the cap and the bottom of the sleeve gradually.

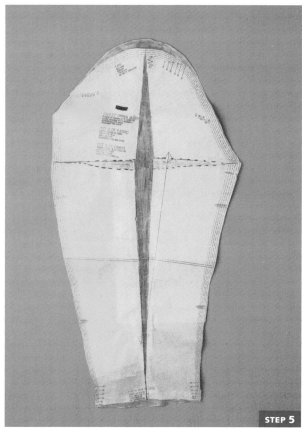

STEP 5

Pull the pattern apart to create a gap. The pattern tissue will overlap a bit horizontally.

TIGHT ARMHOLE

What if your finished clothes and pretest garment all have horizontal wrinkles across the upper portion of the sleeve cap and the sleeve feels tight at the underarm? The problem is that you're long between the armhole and shoulders, which is often troublesome for tall women. The solution is simply to lengthen the bodice and the sleeve between the bottom and the top of the armhole.

1 In the top third of the armhole, draw a horizontal line across the cap of the sleeve pattern piece. Cut the sleeve apart at this line and tape a ½-in. to 1-in. (1.3cm to 2.5cm) extension into the spread. Smooth out the cutting line in the cap without reducing the width.

2 In the same location on the bodice (top third of the armhole), draw a horizontal line across the bodice front and back. Cut the bodice apart at this line and tape in an extension that matches the amount of the sleeve alteration.

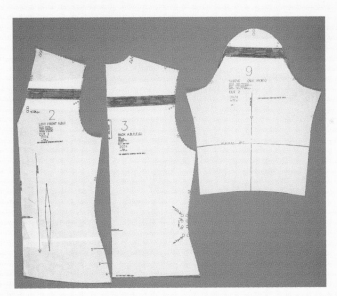

Tight armholes can be remedied by lengthening between the armhole and the shoulder.

6 Redraw the grainline in the middle of the sleeve from shoulder dot to the middle of the bottom of the sleeve. To ease in the extra amount of fabric caused by adding at the top of the sleeve cap, run the easeline all around the sleeve cap rather than just between the notch.

ADD TO BICEPS WITH DESIGN DETAIL

The modern woman often has a larger arm measurement than mainstream patterns allow for, a fact that I discovered while working on the Today's Fit pattern block for Vogue. Many women today work out on a regular basis, giving them wider biceps. To accommodate this change, some well-known designers have reconsidered the way they draft sleeve patterns.

These quality garments avoid tight upper sleeves and instead feature a visible vertical seam as a design detail. Traveling from the cap to hem, this seam can be let out for better fit across muscular arms without increasing fullness in the sleeve cap; it also prevents horizontal wrinkles across the biceps. By adding a vertical seam to a garment you're making, you'll not only increase the size of the sleeve but also create a designer detail by topstitching it. You can even insert piping to give the illusion of a narrower arm.

One-Piece Sleeves

1 Measure the widest part of your biceps and add an additional amount for ease. The amount of ease is purely a personal preference. To determine yours, you can either measure the upper arm width of a few of your favorite garments or use the following amounts: For a jacket or blouse, add 4 in. (10.2cm); for a knit garment, add 1 in. to 2 in. (2.5cm to 5cm).

Creating a seam in a sleeve allows you not only to add in the biceps area without adding at the sleeve cap but also to add a nice design detail at the same time.

2 Take a flat pattern measurement between the seamlines at the corresponding location on your sleeve pattern piece. The difference between your body-plus-ease measurement and the pattern measurement is the amount you need to add.

3 Draw a line on the sleeve pattern from the shoulder dot on the sleeve cap to the bottom of the sleeve on grain. Cut the sleeve apart along this line. Tape a 2-in. (5cm) wide strip of pattern paper to each side. Draw in your alteration where you need it. Put half of your total alteration on each side, tapering off gradually and returning to zero at the sleeve cap seamline to avoid adding extra ease. Add a seam

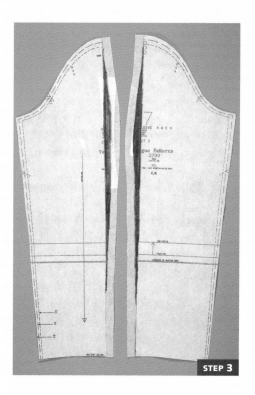

STEP 3

allowance so that the sleeve can be sewn together.

Two-Piece Sleeves

It's just as easy to add a center seamline to a two-piece sleeve.

1 Start by eliminating one of the existing seams—the one closest to the front. Overlap the pattern pieces at the seamlines and tape them together. Depending on the sleeve style, you may have to slash the undersleeve horizontally near the elbow and let it overlap about ¼ in. (6mm) so that the sleeve will lie flat. You can add a bit to the bottom of some sleeve styles so that the seam lengths match.

2 Draw a vertical line through the shoulder placement dot to the bottom of the sleeve on grain. Cut the sleeve pattern piece apart along the new line to make a new two-piece sleeve.

3 Tape a pattern paper extension to the new cut edges on both sleeve pieces. Add half of your total alteration at the widest part of your biceps on each side, tapering to nothing at the shoulder seamline. If your forearm is also full, you may want to maintain your extension all the way to the wrist. Add a seam allowance so that the sleeve can be joined back together.

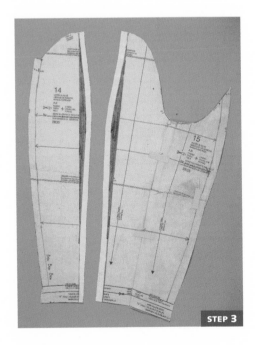

On a two-piece sleeve, one seam can be eliminated and another created, so that the biceps can be expanded without affecting the sleeve cap.

Forward Arm Tilt

THE PROBLEM

If the bone at the top of your arm tilts forward where it joins the shoulder, the result is wrinkles on the front of the sleeve and a collapsed sleeve in back. The alteration for this is quite simple because only the sleeve pattern is involved. The solution is to re-shape the sleeve cap to mimic the shape of your upper arm, but neither the height of the cap nor the amount of ease will be affected. And no change is needed on the bodice armhole.

FAST FIT SOLUTION

Reshape the sleeve by adding to the front of the sleeve cap; reduce the back of the sleeve cap by the same amount. Move the shoulder dot slightly forward. On a two-piece sleeve, tape both pieces together at the sleeve back, and continue the alteration as for a one-piece.

STEP-BY-STEP SOLUTION

1 Outline your size on the sleeve with a marker or highlighter pen.

2 Starting at the top of the sleeve, gradually add ¼ in. (6mm) to the front of the sleeve cap, tapering to zero by the front notch.

3 On the back of the sleeve cap, cut off ¼ in. (6mm), tapering to zero by the back notch.

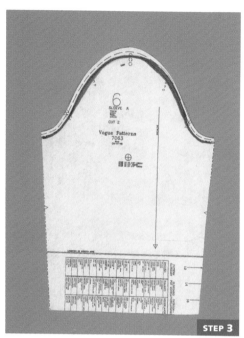

To reshape the sleeve, add to the front of the sleeve cap and reduce the back sleeve cap.

STEP 3

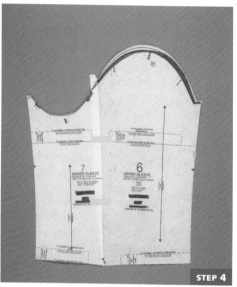

STEP 4

Altering a two-piece sleeve is easier if you overlap one of the underarm seamlines.

Move the shoulder dot forward ¼ in. (6mm) toward the front of the sleeve.

4 On a two-piece sleeve, tape the upper and under sleeve together at the sleeve back with removable tape, near the two notches. Then continue the alteration as though you were working on a one-piece sleeve.

5 Untape the sleeve pieces and cut out the sleeve.

> **FITTING TIP**
>
> You may need to add more than ¼ in. (6mm) to the sleeve front or take out more than ¼ in. (6mm) on the sleeve back. The amount can be refined after testing your first set-in sleeve.

ADDING SLEEVES TO SLEEVELESS STYLES

You finally found the perfect pattern—but it's sleeveless! Can sleeves be added? Absolutely, and without much difficulty. A garment with a sleeve needs additional ease over the bust to allow for arm movement, and the armhole is also slightly lower on a style with a sleeve to allow for the seam allowance. Follow these instructions for a smooth addition.

How to Add a Sleeve

Start with patterns that are the same size: the sleeveless one you want to put a sleeve in and a pattern with a sleeve that you like. Cut off all excess beyond the cutting line for the size you will be using on both patterns. This is important because when you do an overlay, you should be able to see the cutting line clearly.

1 On the sleeveless pattern, tape some extra pattern tissue in the front and back armholes for about 6 in. (15.2cm) down the side seam.

2 Overlay the front of the sleeveless pattern onto the front of the pattern with sleeves. Line up center front, or foldline, and the shoulder cutting line. Do not line up the neckline, because the necks are probably quite different.

3 Trace the armhole of the pattern with the sleeve onto the sleeveless style. (You should be able to see the cutting line of the armhole of the sleeved pattern faintly under the overlay of the sleeveless pattern.) Continue tracing past the armhole down for a few inches into the side seam,

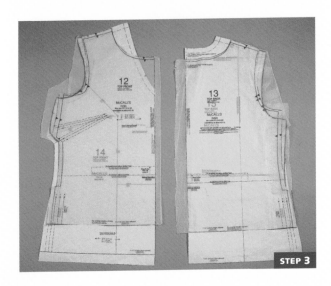

By tracing the armhole of a sleeved pattern onto one without sleeves, it's possible to add sleeves to a sleeveless pattern. Simply line up center front and shoulder cutting lines and start tracing.

STEP 3

tapering back into your sleeveless cutting line gradually. For the sleeve to fit, the armholes must be exactly the same. Mark the front and the back notches of the armhole you will now be using on the added tissue.

4 Once the armholes match, use the new armhole to put in the sleeve.

If sleeveless garments aren't your style, sleeves can be added to just about any sleeveless pattern. The alterations are simple: Lower the armhole and add more ease over the bust area.

DETERMINING SLEEVE SIZE

1 Measure your arm in three key places: right under the armpit, 3 in. (7.6cm) below the armpit, and around the fullest part of the forearm.

2 Add ease to each of these measurements to determine the minimum amount of fabric that a sleeve must have to fit you. Less ease is needed in the forearm area, but this is better determined in the fitting. The minimum movement ease varies by garment:

- 1½ in. (3.8cm) for a close-fitting dress.

- 2½ in. (6.4cm) for a close-fitting jacket or coat.

- 4 in. (10.2cm) for a jacket or coat that will be worn over other garments.

- 1 in. (2.5cm) of ease for garments made from knits or other stretch materials.

These ease amounts are bare minimums. If you are a larger woman, add 1 in. (2.5cm) to all of the above.

Twisted Sleeves

THE PROBLEM

Twisted sleeves, or diagonal wrinkles in the sleeve, not only affect the look of a garment but can also be uncomfortable to wear. The most common cause of these wrinkles is a poor sleeve pattern, one in which the sleeve cap is not high enough. The wrinkles might also indicate a fitting problem: Your upper arm shape does not match the sleeve pattern piece. If your arm thrusts forward or backward you're likely to run into this problem.

If twisted sleeves show up on only some patterns, the problem is in the pattern itself. Some sleeve patterns are designed badly, so don't hesitate to make slight changes. If you're afraid that altering the sleeve cap on your pattern might end up in too much ease, simply follow the instructions in "Reducing Sleeve Ease" on p. 137. The results are worthwhile.

If twisted sleeves show up in every garment you buy or make, then it's a sign of a fitting problem. If this is the case, the solution is simple—you can tackle it after the garment pieces are cut out. At this stage, changes are easy since the side seams are not sewn and machine stitches need only be removed from one sleeve. Pretesting can be particularly useful here; if you pretest nothing else, I strongly suggest pretesting the sleeve pattern. Whether you're creating a new garment or making changes to one already in your closet, this quick procedure is a surefire way to eliminate diagonal wrinkles in the sleeve.

FAST FIT SOLUTION

For pattern problems, raise the height of the sleeve cap. For fitting problems, shift the dot at the top of the sleeve slightly forward or backward until the finished sleeve hangs smoothly. Shift the underarm sleeve seam or placement dot for a two-piece sleeve accordingly.

STEP-BY-STEP SOLUTION

Pattern Problems

1 Raise the height of the sleeve cap by ½ in. (1.3cm), tapering back to the original cutting line by the notches on the sleeve.

Fitting Problems

1 Sew the bodice front and back together at the shoulders and baste the side seams. Baste the underarm seam on one sleeve; don't insert the sleeve yet.

2 Locate the dot at the top and center of the cap on the sleeve pattern piece. This dot indicates where to match the sleeve to the shoulder seam and can be shifted ¼ in. (6mm)

> **FITTING TIP**
> If your shoulders are very narrow, you'll need to alter the bodice before cutting out any of the garment pieces (see "Narrow Shoulders" on p. 108).

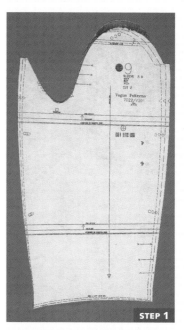

STEP 1

To eliminate a diagonal wrinkle on the sleeve, raise the sleeve cap by ½ in. (1.3cm), tapering back to the original by the notches.

Twisted Sleeves, *continued*

To determine your new shoulder seam placement dot, pivot the dot on the sleeve cap of a pretest garment until the wrinkles are eliminated.

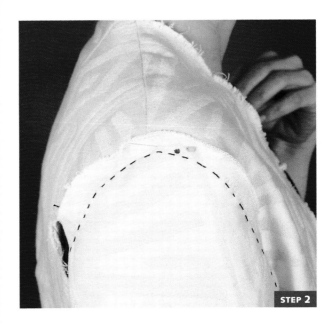

STEP 2

in either direction so that the finished sleeve hangs smoothly. Try on the bodice and then slip the sleeve up your arm. With your arm relaxed, see where the sleeve wants to join the body of the garment. Mark the spot on the sleeve cap that matches the shoulder seam. This is your new shoulder seam placement dot.

3 If you have shifted the dot at the top of the sleeve, shift the underarm sleeve seam or placement dot for a two-piece sleeve accordingly. Pin or baste the sleeve into the corresponding armhole.

4 Try on the garment, and slip in a shoulder pad. If the sleeve is not hanging freely, the sleeve cap may be too shallow. In this case, borrow a little from the sleeve cap seam allowance or add ½ in. (1.3cm) to the top of the cap, tapering to the original cutting line by the notches.

> **FITTING FACT**
>
> **Many European jackets have underarm sleeve seams that are shifted forward as much as ½ in. (1.3cm) so that the sleeves hang properly.**

REDUCING SLEEVE EASE

Too much ease in the sleeve cap screams homemade. Sometimes even the most experienced sewer can't get the smooth results found in a ready-to-wear sleeve. Why? Because patterns often put too much ease in the sleeve cap.

The problem is most common in jackets. If you measure the sleeve from a ready-to-wear jacket and compare it to the jacket armhole, you'll find a sleeve cap ease allowance of ¾ in. to 1¼ in. (1.9cm to 3.2cm). Then, if you measure a jacket sleeve from most jacket patterns and compare it with the armhole, you'll find a sleeve cap ease allowance of 2 in. to 2½ in. (5cm to 6.4cm). A sleeve cap in a ready-to-wear dress or blouse may only have ½ in. (1.3cm) ease, whereas a pattern may have 1 in. to 2 in. (2.5cm to 5cm).

The reason the sewer has difficulty getting ready-to-wear results is because the pattern sleeve has too much ease for the size of the armhole. Sleeve ease can easily be reduced, but the key to doing it correctly depends on accurately measuring both the sleeve and the armhole.

Puckers in the sleeve cap of this jacket are an obvious sign of too much ease. This is a common problem with many patterns, but can easily be corrected with an alteration.

REDUCING SLEEVE EASE (CONTINUED)

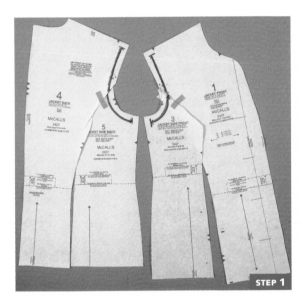

STEP 1

The first step in reducing sleeve ease is to measure the front and back armholes. If the pattern front and back feature two pieces, overlap the seamlines for faster measuring.

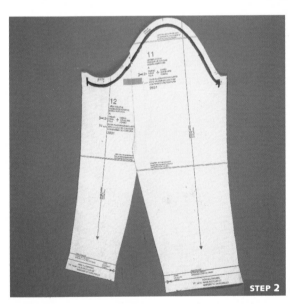

STEP 2

To measure curved seamlines accurately, stand the tape measure on edge.

How to Reduce Sleeve Ease

1 Measure the entire armhole of the jacket, including front, back, and side jacket pieces. Measure only between the seamlines (because we are measuring the actual armhole that the sleeve will go in, seam allowances joining the jacket at the shoulder and side are omitted). If the jacket has a side front and a side back, I find it easier to measure the armhole by turning under one seam allowance and overlapping it onto the next piece, so that the curve of the armhole can be measured continuously.

2 Measure the sleeve, omitting seam allowances. If the sleeve has two pieces to measure, measure the armhole continuously by overlapping the seamline of the upper sleeve onto the seamline of the under sleeve.

3 Compare the two measurements. The sleeve measurement should exceed the armhole measurement by anywhere from ¾ in. to 1¼ in. (1.9cm to 3.2cm). A difficult-to-ease fabric, like wool gabardine, requires ¾ in.

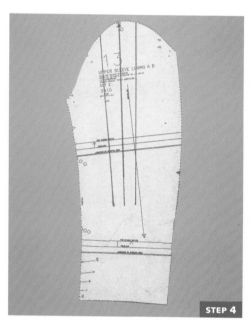

STEP 4

Cut the sleeve pattern apart along three vertical lines from the sleeve cap to the forearm.

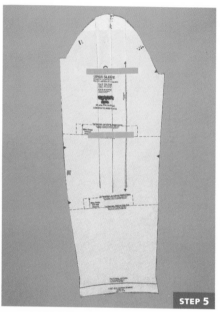

STEP 5

Overlap the sleeve to remove excess ease and smooth out jogs at the top of the sleeve cap, without reducing its height.

(1.9cm) of ease, whereas a normal fabric can take 1¼ in. (3.2cm) of ease. If the difference in measurements is greater than this amount, the sleeve ease should be reduced; if it is within this range, it does not need to be adjusted.

4 To reduce sleeve ease, draw three vertical lines from the top of the sleeve to approximately where the elbow would be: one from the center of the sleeve cap and one on each side, 1½ in. (3.8cm) away. Cut the sleeve pattern apart along all three lines.

5 Divide the total reduction by six, reducing each side of the cut open pattern by one-sixth. For example, to reduce sleeve ease by ¾ in. (1.9cm), overlap the edges of each cut line by ¼ in. (6mm) at the sleeve cap. This reduces ease by ¼ in. (6mm) per cut, and because there are three cuts, a total of ¾ in. (1.9cm) is reduced. Let the overlap diminish to zero as it goes down the sleeve. Smooth out any jogs at the top of the sleeve cap but do not reduce sleeve cap height.

The Neckline

Thick or Thin Neck

THE PROBLEM

The neckline of a garment usually doesn't get much attention beyond the style—until it proves to be uncomfortable. Necklines that are too high, low, tight, or loose not only affect the look of a garment but also our enjoyment wearing them. If you have a particularly thick or thin neck, the drafted pattern piece may position the neckline so that it's not right for your body. A loose or tight neckline is a sure sign that you need to make some changes on your pattern pieces.

It's quite possible for you to have comfortable, flattering necklines on all of your garments, even if they're made from less-than-perfect patterns. The shape and position of your neck will determine the alteration that you need. Regardless of the dilemma, the solutions are easy—simply trimming or adding at the neckline usually does the trick.

FAST FIT SOLUTION

Using a pretest garment, adjust the neck cutting line to the right place—either raise it for a slim neck or lower it for a wider neck. Change the neckline of the garment and facings accordingly, then lengthen or shorten the collar to match.

STEP-BY-STEP SOLUTION

1 Highlight the size you are using on your pattern. Cut out a pretest bodice from scrap fabric and mark the original neck seamline on the fabric pieces. Don't cut out any collar or facing pieces. Sew together the shoulder and side seams.

2 Sew a line of staystitching around the neckline. To adjust for a thin neck, position the stitching $\frac{1}{2}$ in. (1.3cm) from the cut edge. To adjust for a large neck, which needs a wider opening, position the stitching $\frac{3}{4}$ in. (1.9cm) from the cut edge.

3 Clip through the seam allowance to the stitching at 1-in. (2.5cm) intervals around the neckline curve.

FITTING TIP

If the neck is uncomfortable in center front, you may have a forward-thrusting neck. See instructions for this alteration on p. 144.

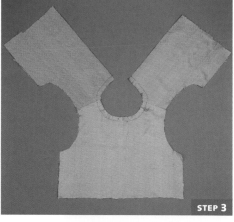

STEP 3

Adjust the neck cutting line by staystitching at $\frac{3}{4}$ in. (1.9cm) for a thick neck and $\frac{1}{2}$ in. (1.3cm) for a thin neck. Clip the neckline curve to the staystitching.

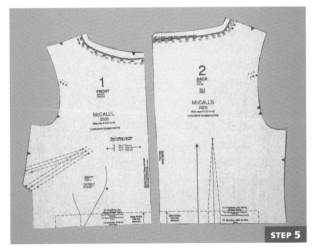

STEP 5

When you've settled on a good fit, trace the new seamline for neckline onto the pattern pieces.

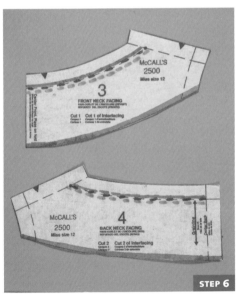

STEP 6

These facings will be altered by the same amount as the neckline alteration.

4 Try on the pretest. If the neckline is still too tight or too loose, sew another row of staystitching $\frac{1}{8}$ in. (3mm) inside or outside of the first row. For a thin neck, you may have to run a line of zigzag stitching to close up the clips. Continue making small adjustments until you're happy with the fit.

5 The line of staystitching is the new neck seamline; transfer it to your front and back pattern pieces.

6 Make the same adjustment at the neckline edge of the facing pattern pieces. Add or subtract the amount of the neckline alteration at the bottom of the facings so they remain the same width.

ADJUSTING A MANDARIN COLLAR

If you have a small neck, a mandarin collar is too wide at the finished edge to conform to the size of your neck, tending to ripple around the neckline near the face. The solution? On the collar piece, draw two or more lines vertically through the collar from the unnotched top edge of the collar to the seamline of the notched edge of the collar. Cut the collar apart along these lines. Overlap the collar tissue ¼ in. to ½ in. (6mm to 1.3cm) at each cut. This reduces the collar circumference two times that amount, since a ¼-in. (6mm) overlap reduces the collar piece by ¼ in. (6mm) and the collar piece represents only half of the collar. No alteration is needed on the neckline of the bodice front and back, because the collar alteration did not affect the collar's neckline edge.

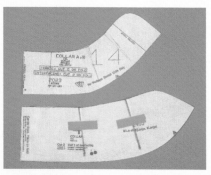

To reduce the circumference on a mandarin collar, make folds in the outside edge and then taper to zero by the neckline edge.

7 Stand a tape measure on edge and measure around the original neck seamline on the pattern piece. Then measure the new seamline (the staystitching) on the garment. The difference between the two measurements is the total alteration for the collar. Since the collar pattern piece represents only half of the collar, divide the total alteration in half to determine the amount to alter the collar pattern piece at center back.

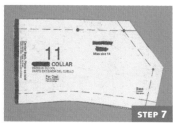

Changes to the neckline size are made at center back on collars.

8 Add or subtract at center back on the collar pattern piece. Ignore the dots and neck notches when sewing on the collar.

Forward-Thrusting Neck

THE PROBLEM

A neckline that rides too high in the front is uncomfortable and unflattering. This is particularly true when the garment has a jewel neckline, with or without a collar. If this is the case on your garments, it's likely that your neck is slightly forward thrusting, which does not allow the neckline to sit at the base of the neck. The solution is easy—cutting off just a bit of fabric from the center front neckline solves the problem.

FAST FIT SOLUTION

Make a pretest garment to determine the right amount to lower the front neckline. Draw a new cutting line on the pattern piece; then alter facings and extend the collar by the same amount.

STEP-BY-STEP SOLUTION

1 Decide how much you want to lower the front neckline. Usually, a drop of ¼ in. to ½ in. (6mm to 1.3cm) will give you a comfortable neckline. You may want to make a pretest bodice and experiment; lower the neck at the center front whatever amount you need to be comfortable.

2 On the front pattern piece, mark the desired drop below the cutting line at center front. Draw a new cutting line from this mark, tapering back to the original neck cutting line as you near the shoulder.

FITTING TIP
Use a French curve for drawing smooth, curved lines on pattern pieces.

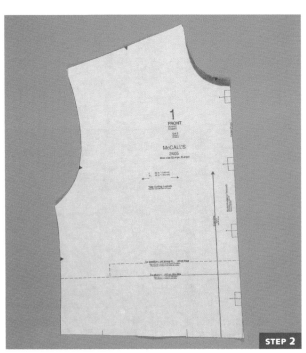

Lower a front neckline to make it more comfortable. Taper back to the original cutting line by the shoulder.

Identical alterations must be made on the front facing. Add the same amount that you lowered the neckline to the bottom of the facing, so that the facing widths remain the same.

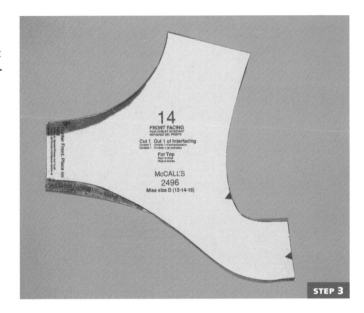

STEP 3

3 If the garment has a front facing, make the same changes on it. Once you lower this neckline edge, it's important to extend the bottom of the facing the same amount. This maintains a uniform facing width and ensures that the facing won't be too skimpy. If the garment doesn't have a collar, your alterations are now complete.

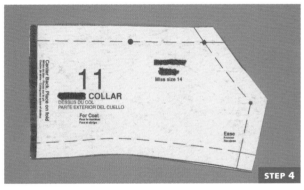

STEP 4

Additions must also be made on the collar at center back.

NECKLINE GAPOSIS

Scoop- or V-neck gaposis is when the neckline stands away from the neck because it doesn't fit properly. It can be eliminated using one of two methods. If the gap is a small amount, deepen the shoulder seams to ⁷⁄₈ in. (2.2cm) at the neckline, tapering back to ⁵⁄₈ in. (1.5cm) by mid-shoulder. This effectively takes out ½ in. (1.3cm) on either side.

More gaposis can be taken out with small slashes, about 3 in. (7.6cm) long, radiating from the neckline. Cut and overlap, taking out no more than ¼ in. (6mm) at each slash. The facings must be adjusted identically.

Neckline gaposis can be eliminated by making small tucks in the neckline; the same should be done on the facings.

4 If the pattern has a collar, stand a tape measure on edge and measure the original front neck seamline. Now measure the new seamline. The difference between the two measurements is the total alteration for the collar. Divide this total alteration in half; because the collar pattern piece represents only half of the collar, this is the amount that you add to the collar pattern piece at center back.

Short Neck

THE PROBLEM

Stand-up collars present a problem for people with short necks. They're a wonderful style, but often the collar is too high, rubbing against your chin and pushing up the hair at the back of your neck. Wouldn't you love to have a long, slim model's neck?

Even with a short neck, you can still look fabulous in a stand-up collar. It's all a matter of proportion—simply change the width of the collar so that it looks right for your body. The finished collar will be more comfortable and in proportion to your neck.

FAST FIT SOLUTION

Determine the amount you want to reduce the collar. At the top of the collar, lower the cutting line the desired amount. The neckline edge does not change, only the top of the collar.

STEP-BY-STEP SOLUTION

1 Decide how much you want to lower the collar. A stand-up collar may need about a ½ in. to ¾ in. (1.3cm to 1.9cm) reduction.

2 At the top of the collar (the unnotched edge, not the neckline edge), measure down the desired amount from the cutting line.

3 Draw a new cutting line. Gradually taper to the original cutting line at both ends of the collar, so that the neckline edge remains the same size.

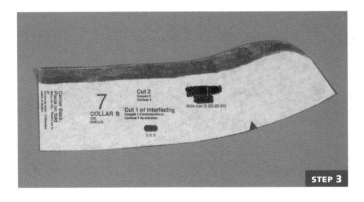

STEP 3

If you have a short neck, you can still wear a stand up collar if you reduce the width. The neckline edge of the collar must remain the same.

The Bust and Upper Body

High or Low Bust

THE PROBLEM

Are you fed up with horizontal wrinkles that appear above or below your bust? On a finished garment, horizontal wrinkles above your bust usually mean that you have a low bust. It can also mean that the cup size of your bra is too small and needs attention as well; if this is the case, see "Good Fit Starts with Your Bra" on p. 155. If the wrinkles appear below your bust, then you have a high bust—very rare indeed.

The solution to this problem often lies in the position of a bust dart. For the smoothest effect, a bust dart should point toward the fullest part of the bust and end 1 in. to $1\frac{1}{2}$ in. (2.5cm to 3.8cm) short of the nipple. But before you can correct this problem, you need to know your bust point or apex—a measurement taken from the middle of the shoulder to the nipple (see "Personal Measurement Chart" on p. 9).

The pattern alteration itself is quite easy. The idea for these instructions came from an ancient sewing book I used in high school, featuring a similar alteration that the instructions called a "bust box."

UP OR DOWN?

Before you decide whether to raise or lower bust shaping, you must locate the apex on your pattern. On the front bodice piece, draw a line through the center of the dart and continuing across the pattern perpendicular to the grainline. If your pattern is size 12 or under, mark an X on the pattern 1 in. (2.5cm) from the end of the dart. If your pattern size is over size 12, mark an X on the pattern 1½ in. (3.8cm) from the end of the dart. This is the apex of the pattern.

Measure the pattern from the middle of the shoulder seamline to the apex. Compare this measurement to your own apex measurement, taken from the middle of your shoulder to the nipple. The difference in measurement between the pattern and you is how much the dart should be lowered or raised for proper positioning.

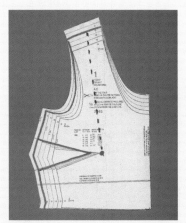

To find the apex of a pattern, draw a line from the center of the shoulder to 1 in. (3.5cm) away from the end of the dart. Compare this to your apex, taken from mid-shoulder to nipple.

FAST FIT SOLUTION

Compare the pattern's apex to your own personal apex measurement; the difference is the amount that the bust dart should be raised or lowered. To do this, make the existing dart into a movable cutout, and shift it up or down on the pattern until it is in the right position.

STEP-BY-STEP SOLUTION

1 Starting at the side seam cutting line on your front pattern piece, draw a straight line diagonally through the middle of the dart. Once you get to the dart point, continue the line perpendicular to the grainline across the pattern to center front.

2 Draw a three-sided box around the existing dart. The box should be just slightly larger than the dart legs and dart length.

3 From the end of the dart to center front, draw a second, parallel line either above or below the first one, where you want the center of the dart to be. The space between the two lines is the amount you want to raise or lower the dart.

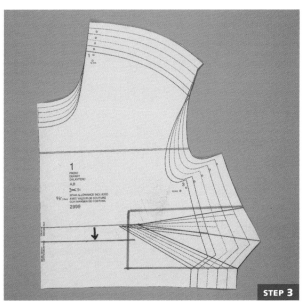

STEP 3

This bodice piece is marked with an arrow and a line to indicate the desired location of the bust dart. A three-sided box is drawn around the existing dart so that it can be moved.

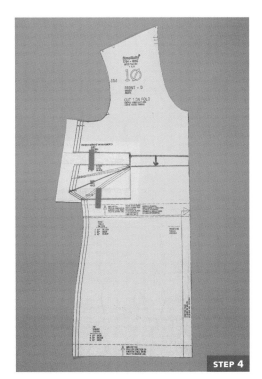

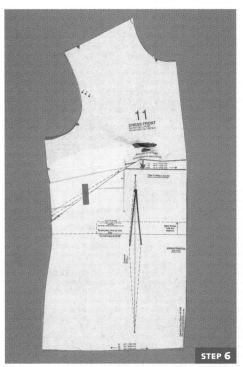

The box can be moved up or down until the centerline of the existing dart matches the line for the new dart position.

Fold out the dart by bringing the bottom dart leg up to meet the top dart leg. Then fold the dart down and recut the side seam.

4 Cut out the three-sided box. Slide it up or down until the centerline of the existing dart matches the line that marks the new dart position. Tape the box in position and fill the empty spot on the pattern piece with extra pattern paper. Tape a little bit of pattern paper on the side so that you can correctly position the dart extension.

5 Fold out the dart by bringing the bottom line of the dart up to meet the top line on the dart. Fold the dart down toward the waist on the pattern. Redraw the side seam cutting line and cut away excess to properly reshape the dart at the side seam.

> **FITTING FACT**
>
> Horizontal buttonholes begin ⅛ in. (3mm) away from center front; vertical buttonholes are at center front.

LOW BUST AND PRINCESS SEAMS

Being a B cup doesn't ensure a perfect fit for every garment. If your bust is low, the princess curves on the front and center front pattern pieces will be too high, creating extra fabric above the bust and a snug fit right over the full bust. This is an easy problem to resolve, and requires adjusting only the side front pattern piece. It may take a bit of experimentation, but you'll see that it works.

On the side front, draw a straight line across the pattern at the bottom of the armhole cutting line. Measure the amount below this line that you want to lower the curve and draw another line parallel to the first. The placement of this second line indicates where you want the fullest part of the curve to be. Trim off some of the curve above and below the first line. Take the curve you cut off and shift it down until the first line matches the second line; tape it to the pattern. Now, your body's curves exactly match the pattern's fullness at the bust.

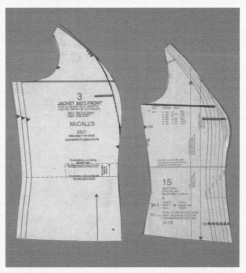

The bust curve can be easily shifted to a new, lower position. Simply draw a horizontal line on the side front piece at the bottom of the armhole, and another line at the new location. Cut off the curve between the lines and shift it down so that the first line on the outer curve matches up with the second on the bodice.

6 If the pattern also has a vertical dart, simply raise or lower the end of the bust dart on the pattern the same amount you moved the horizontal dart. Redraw the dart sewing lines to connect so that the end of the dart finishes smoothly with the minimum amount of fabric at the end.

GOOD FIT STARTS WITH YOUR BRA

When it comes to good garment fit, never underestimate the importance of properly fitting undergarments. For any bust alteration, it's especially important that you start with an accurate cup size because your bra fit ultimately affects the way a garment fits in the bust area. A well-fitting bra straightens out bulges and eliminates the rolls created by a bra that is too tight—a garment cannot hang smoothly over bulging foundations. If you're spilling out over the top or sides, there's a good chance that you need a bigger cup. If your bust does not fill in the cup completely with smooth, unwrinkled fabric over the cups, the cup size is too big. So before you even begin making alterations on your garment, carefully in-spect the fit of your bra. Some brands fit better than others; Lily of France, in par-ticular, gives a nice smooth line, espe-cially on a large bust.

Today many high-quality department stores have fit specialists to help you find the size and style of bra that's most flat-tering and comfortable. If you're measur-ing yourself, fitting teacher Eileen Lucas from Design and Sew offers the following technique: Measure yourself around your full bust and right under your bustline around the rib cage. Every 1 in. (2.5cm) of difference between the two measure-ments determines an additional cup size. For example, if you measure 36 in. (91cm)

under the bust and 39 in. (99cm) around your full bust, the 3-in. (7.6cm) difference indicates three sizes up in cup size; in other words, your correct bra size would be a 36C. Once you are properly fitted you'll be pleasantly surprised to discover that not only have you banished the bulges around the edges of your bra but your clothes fit better, too.

Bra size greatly affects garment fit. This bra is obviously too small and will cause bumps and bulges to show on outer garments.

Large Bust

THE PROBLEM

If you have a large bust, you may find that the front of your garments are sometimes shorter than the back. A pleat starting at the armhole and traveling toward the bust indicates that the garment is not full enough in the bust area.

Women with large busts often get frustrated with alterations. The most common alteration, adding at the side seams, doesn't always do the trick. It may provide enough circumference in the bust area, but the fit still isn't perfect: Instead, the front hikes up and you're left with giant armholes. Don't despair—there are better solutions.

There are two ways to improve bust fit. One option is to adjust the size of the bust dart (see "Changing Dart Size" on p. 166). The second option is to cut the pattern apart and spread it to the desired size, a technique that I learned from Tedde Motecka, a skilled pattern grader who worked with me on the Today's Fit patterns for Vogue. The beauty of both of these techniques is that they don't change the size of the armhole, so no changes are needed on the sleeve. Personally, I prefer the second method, which is outlined here, because wider darts can be difficult to end smoothly.

FAST FIT SOLUTION

On the front pattern piece, draw two lines: one from the center of the shoulder to the bust point, and another from the bust point to the bottom of the bodice. Slash and spread the pattern along these lines to get the desired circumference. Additional cuts between the armhole and the spreading line are adjusted to allow the pattern to lie flat.

STEP-BY-STEP SOLUTION

1 On the front pattern piece, draw a line from the center of the shoulder to the bust point (line A). The bust point is 1 in. to 1$\frac{1}{2}$ in. (2.5cm to 3.8cm) from the end of the dart. Draw a second line, parallel to the grainline, from the bust point to the bottom of the bodice (line B).

2 Draw three more or less evenly spaced diagonal lines from the front armhole to line A, in the area between the bust point and the shoulder.

3 Cut the pattern apart along lines A and B. Then, cut almost completely through all of the diagonal lines, stopping $\frac{1}{8}$ in. (3mm) from the armhole cutting line. Place the pattern pieces on a flat surface over a piece of tissue paper.

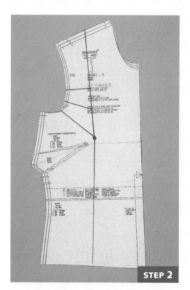

STEP 2

Draw lines from mid-shoulder to the apex and to the bottom of the bodice. Draw three lines from the armhole that intersect with this line above the apex.

FITTING TIP

A large bust often creates a hollow just above the bust. To avoid this, take a ¼-in. (6mm) horizontal pleat—½ in. (1.3cm) total—out of the front neckline on the pattern. Smooth the pleat into obscurity.

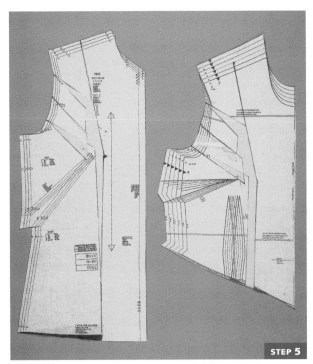

STEP 5

This pattern piece has been spread vertically. The pieces overlap and spread apart at each of the horizontal lines so that the pattern lies flat.

4 Depending on how much circumference you need, spread the pattern apart ½ in. to 1½ in. (2.5cm to 3.8cm) at the bust point. Spread or close the rest of the cut shapes as necessary to keep the pattern flat. If you need it, spread the pattern apart a bit at the waist, or taper in to its original position.

5 Tape the adjusted pattern piece to the tissue paper underneath and smooth out the cutting line on the bottom.

LARGE BUST AND PRINCESS SEAM ADJUSTMENTS

Right out of the envelope, a standard American pattern has a B cup. If your bust is any larger, you may have garments that pull up at center front or have taut horizontal wrinkles form across the bust area. Princess seams can help to solve these problems, offering the best fit for a large bust. Instead of one front piece, a princess seam divides the front into two pieces, providing more opportunities to alter. The seams that join front and side front pattern pieces mimic the curves of your body. In this case, the bust curve can be increased in small increments to make room for a larger bust.

But don't stop with this adjustment. The front pattern piece should also be altered, or the seamline will ripple because the garment pieces aren't the same size. For a larger bust with a larger bust curve, the front must be lengthened so that the seam length matches the new, larger side front bust curve. As a result, your finished garment won't ride up at center front.

1 Draw a horizontal line across the side front, perpendicular to the grainline, 1 in. (2.5cm) down from the armhole cutting line on the side front.

2 On this line, cut the pattern from the bust curve to the seamline of the side cutting line. Clip into the seam allowance slightly to relax the tissue; this makes a "hinge" for your alteration.

3 Spread the top of the side front apart at the bust cutting line ½ in. (1.3cm) for every cup size beyond B. Taper the spread to nothing at the side seam. Keep the original grainline from under the bust adjustment down as your new grainline.

4 On the front pattern piece, make a length adjustment the same amount as the increase at the bust curve on the side front. The alteration is made in the corresponding spot, but added all the way across the pattern. Match up the seams at the armhole to determine where to cut the front piece apart.

5 Alter the front facing and the lining the same way.

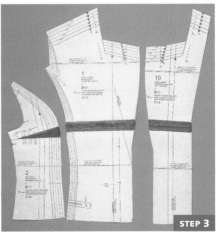

On princess styles, increase the length ½ in. (1.3cm) for every cup size beyond a B.

Full Bust Gaposis

THE PROBLEM

Even if you adjust your pattern for a generous full bust or tummy, your finished jacket or vest can still have a fit problem, especially if the full bust is accompanied by a protruding tummy. In this case, even if you've altered for a full bust, the front edges of your jackets and vests still open out at an angle from the bust, rather than hanging straight. If this sounds familiar, the following alteration is for you.

Fit expert Gale Grigg Hazen, author of *Fantastic Fit for Every Body,* calls this problem "gaposis." It can be corrected with a simple pattern alteration. The following instructions are intended for a pattern with a one-piece front, but they work just as easily on a pattern that has front and side front pattern pieces. All other pattern alterations should be made first so that the grainline will remain intact.

FAST FIT SOLUTION

Take a horizontal tuck out of center front, tapering to zero by the side seam. This brings the lower front in so it hangs vertically rather than at an angle on the body.

STEP-BY-STEP SOLUTION

1 Just under the bust, draw a horizontal line across the pattern from the front edge to the side seam.

2 Fold out ½ in. (1.3mm) at the front edge, tapering to zero at the side seamline.

3 Redraw the grainline using the above-the-fold grainline for reference. Straighten out the front edge with a ruler, smoothing out any jogs along the front edge formed by folding up the pattern.

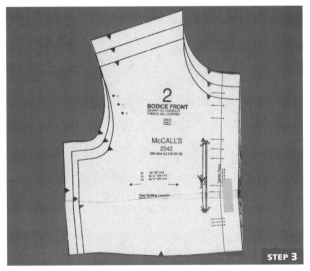

Prevent front gaposis by folding out ½ in. (5cm) horizontally below the bust, tapering to zero by the side seam. Smooth out the front edge, filling in the missing section.

FITTING TIP
Scrutinize the garment's opening. If it buttons at the center front, the center front markings should match exactly. If you can't match the center fronts, you may need to let out the side seams a bit or you won't be able to button up the garment. On jackets, remember that interfacing and lining take up extra space.

MOVING A BUST DART

In some cases, rather than lowering or raising a bust dart you may want to move it altogether for a more flattering effect. And sometimes you may want to hide a dart under the lapel, move the dart bulk out of a pocket, or simply give your bust an illusion of lift. Moving a bust dart is very easy to do.

Draw in a new dart line at the desired location, starting at the waistline, side seam, or mid-shoulder and ending at the apex. Cut along this line. The dart itself should end 1½ in. (3.8cm) from the apex to make room for the bust, but the pattern must be cut to the apex.

On the old dart, cut along the lower line of a horizontal dart or the dart line closest to center front of a vertical dart. Close up the old dart by bringing the dart legs together, and tape it in place. The opening formed by the cut on the new line is the new dart. Draw in the new dart legs, which correspond to the opening in the paper; remember to end the dart 1½ in. (3.8cm) from the apex. Fold the new dart legs together to obtain the cutting line for the seam.

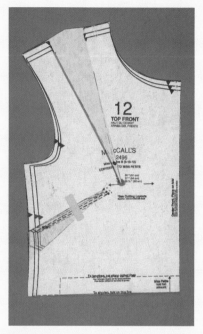

Darts can be relocated by cutting a new opening and closing up the old dart.

4 On a style with a front and side front, draw a line horizontally across both the front and side front, just under the bust. On the front piece fold out ½ in. (1.3mm) at center front, tapering to ¼ in. (6mm) by the side front cutting edge. On the side front piece, fold out ¼ in. (6mm) on the side front cutting line, tapering to zero by the side seam.

Small Bust

THE PROBLEM

Women with a small bust have just as many fitting problems as those with a large bust. A small bust results in too much fullness in a garment, which then collapses at the bustline. Princess seams often create extra fullness because they have too much curve and too much length for the small bust. But the curve in the seam can be reduced to eliminate all of the extra fabric. American patterns are designed for a B cup, so if your cup size is smaller you will need a pattern alteration to get the look you want.

FAST FIT SOLUTION

To decrease the fullness in a princess seam, the center front piece must be shortened. The side front piece will be hinged so that the front curve is slightly collapsed, resulting in a closer fit over the bust.

STEP-BY-STEP SOLUTION

1 On the side front pattern piece, mark 1 in. (2.5cm) down from the armhole cutting line, or at the place where the princess curve is the most pronounced. Draw a horizontal line through this point across the pattern piece, perpendicular to the grainline.

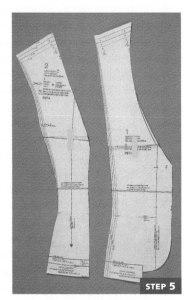

STEP 5

To reduce the bust by a cup size on a princess line, fold out a small amount on the center front piece and on the side front, tapering to zero by the side seam.

2 Cut the pattern on this line all the way to the seamline of the side cutting line. Make a clip in the seam allowance to relax the pattern tissue. Note that this makes a hinge for your alteration.

3 Overlap the top and bottom of the pattern along the cut line by ½ in. (1.3cm), tapering to the original side seam cutting line. This reduces the bust by ½ in. (1.3cm), or one cup size. Tape the pieces together and smooth out any jogs on the side front seam.

4 Make a length adjustment on the front pattern piece the same amount as the reduction in the bust curve on the side front. For example, for an A cup, fold out ½ in. (1.3mm) horizontally across the entire front pattern piece. To do this, draw a line across the front of the pattern in the same place as the one on the side front. The location of notches, if there are any, can be helpful. Draw another line ½ in. (1.3cm) below the first; then fold out the excess ½ in. (1.3cm) by bringing the lines together. Tape the pieces together and smooth out the cutting line on the front edge of the pattern.

5 Alter the front facing and front lining by the same amount and at the same location as the front pattern piece.

CREATING A PRINCESS SEAM

If you have a figure with a lot of curves or a hollow above the bust, adding a princess seam from shoulder to hem will give you more flexibility for a smoother fit. Instead of one front piece, a princess seam divides the front into two pieces, giving us more opportunities to alter by taking in or letting out the princess seams as well as the side seams. Here's how to create a princess seam.

1 Place a dot on the bodice front at the apex, 1½ in. (1.3cm) from the end of the horizontal dart. (If there is no dart, see "Up or Down?" on p. 151 to determine the apex.)

2 Halfway across the shoulder, draw in a new line to the apex. Draw another line from the apex to the bottom of the garment, perpendicular to the grainline. This line will become your new seamline.

3 Cut open the pattern on the new seamline from the bottom of the bodice to the apex.

4 On the existing dart line, cut along the bottom dart leg from the side to the apex. Eliminate the dart by bringing up the bottom leg of the dart to the top leg of the dart; tape the dart closed. As you close up the dart, the pattern spreads apart at the bottom. If the pattern has no dart, eliminate this step.

5 Continue cutting the pattern apart vertically from the apex to the shoulder to create a front and side front piece. Label the pieces "front" and "side front." Add seam allowances to both sides of your cutting line. Smooth out the cutting line on the side front bust curve. Voilà! You've successfully created a princess seam.

Create a princess seam by drawing in style lines and closing up darts.

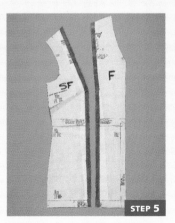

To create a princess seam, cut the bodice front pattern piece completely apart and add seam allowances.

Gaping Armholes

THE PROBLEM

No matter what size your bust is, vests, jumpers, and sleeveless dresses have an annoying tendency to gape at the armhole because the bust pulls the bodice away from the armhole. This problem can be even worse on women with a large bust.

The solution is to reduce the circumference of the armhole near the seamline, which encourages the garment to conform to the curves of your body. A simple way to do this is by running an easeline on the front armhole. The amount of ease depends on your bust size: Ease in $\frac{1}{8}$ in. (3mm) for an A cup, $\frac{1}{4}$ in. (6mm) for a B cup, $\frac{3}{8}$ in. (1cm) for a C cup, $\frac{1}{2}$ in. (1.3cm) for a D cup, and $\frac{5}{8}$ in. (1.5cm) for a DD cup. (Use these amounts as guidelines only; personally, I rarely measure how much I am easing.) Some fabrics may not ease well, such as faux leather, suede, or upholstery-weight fabrics, so you may need to reduce the amount of ease depending on the fabric.

FAST FIT SOLUTION

To bring the armhole closer to the body, run an easeline on the front armhole. Lock the ease into place with a stabilizer and continue construction.

STEP-BY-STEP SOLUTION

1 Using a stitch length of 3.0mm (4.0mm for heavy fabric), run an easeline on the front of the armhole. Fabric can be eased either by pulling the bobbin thread slightly after sewing, or by pushing at the back of the presser foot. Keeping the easeline within the seam allowance, sew about ½ in. (1.3cm) away from the edge of the fabric.

2 Additional shaping along the front V-neck of a vest is possible by running an easeline along the front neckline. Your goal is to take out between ¼ in. and ⅜ in. (6mm and 1cm) in length.

3 If you think you may not have eased enough, measure the armhole before and after the easing by holding the tape measure on edge along the curve of the armhole.

4 Once you have eased the desired amount, stabilize the armhole by sewing twill tape or a piece of narrow selvage over your easelines. Press so that the area has contours but no obvious puckers at the seamline.

5 If you have a rounded back, the same principle can be used to enable the back armhole to better conform to the body. For a rounded back, ease the entire back armhole.

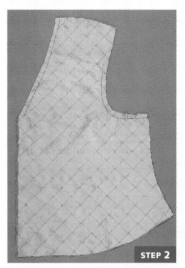

STEP 2

To prevent armholes from gaping, run an easeline within the seam allowance in the lower two thirds of the armhole. Also run an easeline along the front of a V-neck.

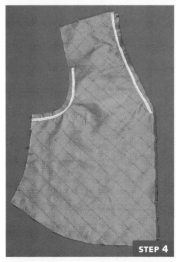

STEP 4

Stabilize the easeline by sewing or pressing on twill tape.

REPLACING BUTTONHOLES WITH LOOPS

If you prefer loops instead of button-holes in your garment, avoid attaching the loops in the seam on the garment's front edge—this throws the opening off-center. Instead, create a seam at the center front between the front and the front facing and insert the loops in this seam. Prevent garments from showing underneath by attaching a small placket in the seam on the opposite side. Here's how to make the placket.

1 Cut a piece of fabric approximately 3½ in. (8.1cm) wide and 18 in. (46cm) long, or long enough to lie behind the buttons from top to bottom. The length and width of the strips should be determined by the number of loops and the width of the button.

2 With right sides together, sew the short ends.

3 Trim the seam; turn right side out and press.

4 Line up the raw edges of the placket with the raw edge of the front of the garment. The finished end of the placket should be ⅞ in. (2.2cm) from the cut edge of the neckline, and it should extend 1 in. (2.5cm) beyond the last button. Sew facing to the front, with the raw ends of the placket sandwiched in between.

Prevent undergarments from showing behind button loops with a placket inserted along the front edge, between the front and the front facing.

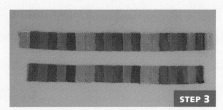

STEP 3

With right sides together, sew the short ends of the placket piece and press the seams open. Trim seams to ¼ in. (6mm); turn right side out and press.

Mastectomy

THE PROBLEM

If you have had a mastectomy, the two front halves of your body are no longer the same size. Without any alterations, a garment will look fuller on one side and collapse above the bust on the small side, creating wrinkles and making the difference more obvious. A simple alteration to your pattern can correct this problem; so well, in fact, that the difference won't even be noticeable once the pattern is altered.

The solution involves altering only one side of the garment, so it will no longer be possible to cut double fronts and sleeves. Each side of the pattern and the sleeve must be cut separately.

FAST FIT SOLUTION

Make a copy of the pattern pieces for the bodice and sleeve, so that alterations can be made on only one side. Remove a total of $^1/_2$ in. (1.3cm) from the flat side of the bodice, overlapping the pattern pieces by $^1/_2$ in. (1.3cm) in the armhole. Do the same on the corresponding sleeve between the shoulder and the bottom of the armhole.

STEP-BY-STEP SOLUTION

1 Make a copy of the pattern pieces for the bodice and the sleeve, so that each side can be altered separately. Label the pieces "left" and "right."

2 On the smaller, flatter side of the bodice between the shoulder and the bottom of the armhole, draw a line across the bodice perpendicular to the grainline. Cut along this line from the armhole to the front edge, leaving the pattern intact from the seamline at the side front or front edge.

3 To remove a total of $\frac{1}{2}$ in. (1.3cm), overlap the pattern pieces $\frac{1}{2}$ in. (1.3cm) in the armhole. If the front is cut in one piece, let the fold taper to zero as it approaches the middle of the bodice piece. If the front is cut in two pieces,

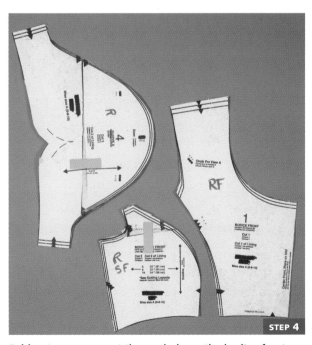

STEP 4

Fold out any excess at the armhole on the bodice front and the sleeve on the small side only.

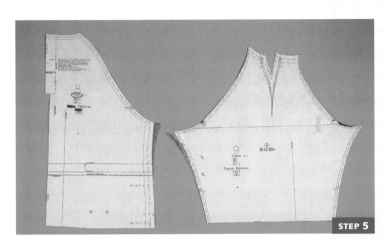

Extra fullness under the back armhole can be camouflaged by adding at the side seam on both the bodice back and the underarm seam in back.

STEP 5

taper the fold to zero as it approaches the end of the side front piece. Tape in place, and smooth out the armhole curve on the front bodice.

4 On the sleeve that corresponds to this side, between the shoulder and the bottom of the armhole, draw a horizontal line across the pattern perpendicular to the grainline. Cut along this line, leaving the pattern intact from the seamline to the cutting line on the back of the sleeve. Overlap the front of the sleeve ½ in. (1.3cm)–to remove a ½-in. (1.3cm) total– letting the overlap reduce to zero halfway across the sleeve. Tape in place and smooth out the armhole curve on the sleeve piece.

5 You may find it difficult to get a smooth line under the back armhole because of extra body fullness between the armhole and the waist in back. In this case, add to the back bodice on the side seam right under the arm-hole, tapering to the original cutting line by the waist. An addition must also be made to the back underarm on the sleeve for the sleeve to fit in the armhole properly.

> **FITTING TIP**
>
> To give the concave, flatter side a bit more support, underline it with silk organza. On a jacket, use a chest shield with extra padding on the concave side.

The Rounded Body

THE PROBLEM

A rounded body—large bust combined with fullness around the waist area—causes several fitting problems. Garments tend to pull away from the armhole, forming a dart crease radiating from the armhole. The bodice is not comfortable, rising up over the bust and forming a horizontal fold above the bust, and the fronts don't hang straight and tend to hike up, spreading to accommodate the larger circumference and the larger cup size.

While these problems may seem unrelated, they are not. In fact, they can all be eliminated with one pattern alteration that will give you more circumference around the bust and waist, and more length to prevent the bodice from hiking up. Also, if your pattern does not already have a front dart, adding one will give the garment more shape, enabling it to go over curves smoothly and hang closer to the body.

FAST FIT SOLUTION

Slash and spread the pattern both vertically and horizontally to add length and width at the bottom edge of the garment. If your pattern does not have a dart, add a dart the same size as the amount of the addition at the bust area; if the pattern already has a dart, widen it by the amount of the vertical pattern spread at the side seam.

STEP-BY-STEP SOLUTION

1 Draw a vertical line on the pattern from mid-shoulder to the bottom of the pattern.

2 If your pattern has a dart, draw a horizontal line through the center of the dart and continue it across the pattern perpendicular to the grainline. If your pattern doesn't have a dart, draw a horizontal line across the pattern 2 in. (5cm) down from the armhole.

3 Cut the pattern apart vertically from the bottom of the bodice to within ¼ in. (6mm) of the shoulder cutting line. Don't cut completely through the pattern at the shoulder; leave this as a hinge.

4 Next, cut horizontally across the pattern, leaving nothing intact. Place the pattern pieces over tissue paper on a flat surface.

5 Add ¾ in. to 1 in. (1.9cm to 2.5cm) or more to the pattern horizontally.

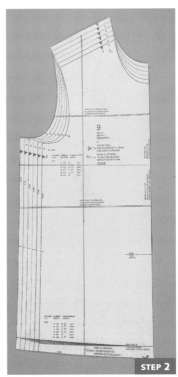

STEP 2

A rounded body needs both length and width at the bottom edge of the garment. Slash and spread the pattern both vertically and horizontally.

Cut through the center of the dart and then perpendicular to the grainline toward the center; cut vertically from the hem to the shoulder seamline. Spread the pattern, adding as much as you need.

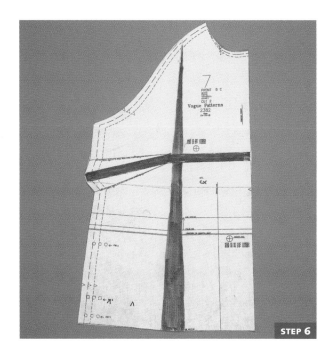

STEP 6

6 Spread the pattern apart vertically at the bottom edge of the bodice for additional circumference. To avoid adding width to the shoulder, the addition should taper to zero at the top. Leave the center fronts in line, keeping the grainline intact, spreading the side panels. Add as much as you need. Tape the pattern to the tissue paper underneath.

7 If the pattern does not have a dart, draw in a dart the width of the addition to provide shape and contour to the front of the garment. End the dart 1 in. (2.5cm) from the bust point. If the pattern originally had a dart, widen the dart the amount of the vertical pattern spread at the side seam.

8 Use the original grainline when cutting out. Experiment on scrap fabric to refine the amounts of length and width to what your body requires.

Buttoning over a Large Tummy

THE PROBLEM

If you have trouble buttoning jackets, vests, or anything else fitted that buttons (and you refuse to give up desserts, like me!), it's likely you already know what the problem areas are: your tummy, a full high hip, and probably a fleshy back as well. Trying to button these garments often results in a sculpted effect that is not very flattering.

The solution requires a subtle addition of extra fabric over these problem areas, without distorting the style of the garment. For starters, you need to find out how much fabric is necessary to cover the area without getting that sculpted effect—the reason most of us have given up buttoning jackets and vests in the first place. The beauty of the following technique is that no other alteration is needed except on the lining. It involves the side pattern pieces only and adds nothing to the center front and center back panels. When you're finished, you'll finally be able to button your vests and jackets.

FAST FIT SOLUTION

Determine the amount of alteration necessary by comparing your high hip measurement plus ease to the flat pattern measurement on the pattern in the same area. Divide this total alteration amount by either two or four, depending on the number of side pattern pieces you're working with. Slash and spread each of the side panels by this amount.

STEP-BY-STEP SOLUTION

1 Take your high hip measurement 3 in. (7.6cm) down from the waist. (This measurement is also called the tummy measurement; see your "Personal Measurement Chart" on p. 9.) If most of your fullness is above the waist, measure that area as well. Work with the largest of the two measurements.

2 On your pattern piece, highlight the size you usually use as a point of reference. Then measure down 3 in. (7.6cm) from the pattern waist or above the waist, if you are fullest there. Draw a line across the pattern pieces with stop marks at the seam allowances and the center front. The stop marks will remind you not to measure into the seam allowances.

3 Pin out any darts and pleats. Measure all of the pattern pieces between the seamlines. Do not measure beyond center front.

<hr>

FITTING TIP

If you work primarily at a desk and would like to have your jacket buttoned while sitting, measure yourself sitting down. This measurement is often bigger than the standing hip measurement.

4 Add all of these measurements and multi-ply the total by two, since the pattern pieces will be cut double. This figure represents how many inches of fabric are available to you once the jacket is made up. Write it down and label this amount "have."

5 To your body measurement above or below the waist, add 3 in. (7.6cm) of ease for a vest, 5 in. (12.7cm) for a jacket, and 6 in. to 8 in. (15.2cm to 20.3cm) for a coat. Label this amount "need" (see the ease charts on p. 29 for specifics). Compare your "need" figure to the "have" figure–the difference is the alteration amount.

6 If the pattern has a side front and a side back, divide the total alteration by four; this is the amount added to the side front and side back, which will be cut double. If the pattern has only one side pattern piece, divide the alteration by two, since the piece will be cut double.

7 On each side panel, draw a vertical line parallel to the grainline from 2 in. (5cm) below the armhole (if the fullness is below the waist)–or from the armhole (if the fullness is above the waist)–to the bottom of the jacket or vest.

8 If the line ended below the armhole, continue by angling the line back into the side seam. If your fullness is higher, begin under the bust, angling the line back into the bottom of the armhole.

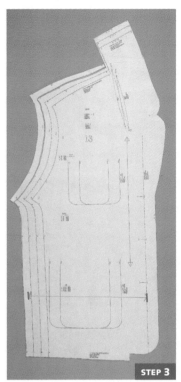

STEP 3

To create a garment that buttons easily over a large tummy, start by taking flat pattern measurements of all pattern pieces in your fullest area between the seamlines. No measurements go beyond the center front.

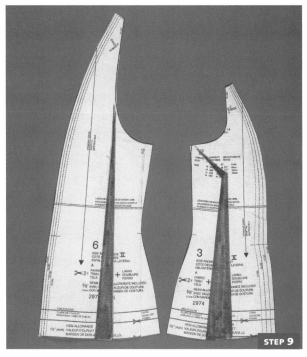

STEP 9

When your vests and jackets no longer button, an easy adjustment can be made on side front and side back by merely spreading them the amount you need.

> **FITTING TIP**
>
> **When using the slash-and-spread technique, slashes should stop at the seamline, not the cutting line. A small cut into the seam allowance enables the pattern to lie flat.**

9 Cut the pattern apart along these lines to the seam allowance near the edge; leave the pattern intact for ¼ in. (6mm) near the armhole so that it doesn't fall apart completely. Spread the pattern the amount needed for the alteration. For example, if you need to add 3 in. (7.6cm) total and you have both a side front and a side back piece, divide the total by four and add a ¾-in. (1.9cm) spread on each side piece. If your pattern has only one side panel, divide your alteration by two and add 1½ in. (3.8cm) to each side panel.

10 Tape the pattern to tissue paper and smooth out the jogs along the bottom cutting line. Use your original grainline for cutting reference.

Narrow Upper Chest

THE PROBLEM

As we age, women often become narrower in the upper chest. As a result, choosing a pattern size by the high bust or full bust measurements can lead to disappointment. If you choose a size based on your high bust measurement, the remainder of the bodice—and the entire back—are too tight. On the other hand, using your full bust measurement to choose a pattern size works for most areas, with the exception of the upper chest—the front above the armhole. Between the two, the full bust measurement is a better choice for making a minimum amount of alterations.

Even with the right size, you'll most likely need to alter in the front upper chest area. Otherwise, the shoulder seams drop off the shoulder, and the neckline won't rest flat against the body. The following alterations will reduce the width of the front chest, which also changes the shape of the armhole and requires a front sleeve adjustment to match.

FAST FIT SOLUTION

Reduce the front chest width above the armhole only. Because the size of the armhole seam will change, you'll also need to alter the sleeve front to match the new armhole shape. Compare front and back shoulder lengths; either add an easeline or draw in a dart to accommodate the difference in length.

STEP-BY-STEP SOLUTION

1 Put on a finished garment that's too large in the upper front chest, but fits otherwise, and stand in front of a mirror. On one side of the garment pin a vertical fold from shoulder to bust that pulls the shoulder seam into proper position at the top of the arm. Remove the garment and measure the width of the fold, which usually ranges from $\frac{1}{2}$ in. to $1\frac{1}{2}$ in. (1.3cm to 3.8cm). This is the right amount to reduce the upper chest.

2 On the front pattern piece, draw a horizontal line from the bottom of the armhole toward center front, stopping about midway across the shoulder.

3 Draw a vertical line from the shoulder to the horizontal line at the bottom of the armhole. Away from the first line in the direction of the armhole, draw another vertical line the amount you want to reduce the width, as determined in Step 1.

FITTING TIP

If the fabric is soft and pliable, an easeline on the back is not necessary. Simply sew the front and back shoulders together with the start and ends matching and the back shoulder closest to the feed dogs. The machine feed dogs will ease the bottom layer to fit the shorter front.

---

4 At the bottom of the armhole, cut horizontally through the pattern to the vertical line that is closest to center front. This cut in the pattern allows you to fold out the excess pattern paper without affecting the area below the armhole.

5 Fold out the excess, the total alteration, by bringing the two vertical lines together. Tape the pattern together again.

6 After shifting the detached section of the pattern piece toward center front, the armhole seam becomes longer. To match up the sleeve with the new armhole, add the same amount that was taken out of the front pattern piece to the front sleeve. To do this, add a pattern paper extension to the front underarm seam on the sleeve pattern piece.

7 At the bottom of the armhole, measure out the same amount as the upper chest alteration. Extend the cutting line of the front armhole to this mark, then draw a new cutting line down the underarm seam, tapering to the original cutting line 5 in. to 7 in. (12.7cm to 17.8cm) down. Fold the sleeve in half vertically.

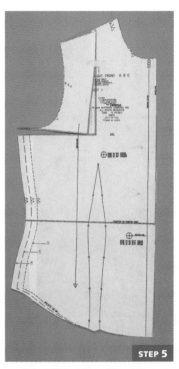

STEP 5

To reduce the width of the front chest, make a horizontal cut at the bottom of the armhole, halfway across the pattern. Fold out the excess in the front and upper chest.

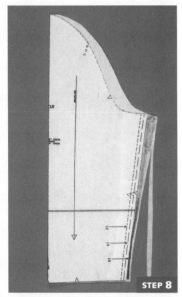

STEP 8

To prevent the sleeve from twisting when one side of it is altered, cut a bit off the sleeve back to match the cutting line on the front. As a result, the circumference is not altered and the sleeve is in balance.

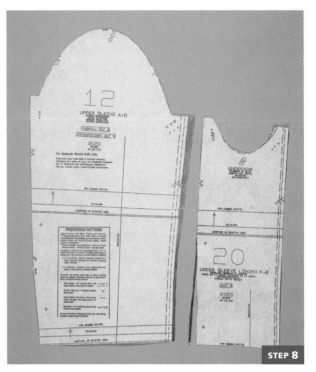

STEP 8

The sleeve must be balanced at the bottom by adding slightly to the upper sleeve and reducing some from the under sleeve.

8 To keep the sleeve from twisting and the circumference at the bottom of the sleeve the same size, you may have to add a bit to the bottom front of the sleeve and cut off a bit from the bottom back of the sleeve. The sleeve circumference at the bottom remains the same, but the sleeve seam won't twist on the body. On a two-piece sleeve, make this alteration on the front underarm sleeve pattern piece.

GIANT BUTTON FORMULA

If you are using larger buttons than the pattern calls for, you may need to extend the front edge of the pattern to accommodate them. Here's a good rule of thumb that's useful for making this determination: The distance from the finished edge of the garment to the center front must equal the diameter of the button. For example, if your buttons are 2 in. (5cm) in diameter, your finished extension past center front should be 2 in. (5cm). Extend the pattern before you cut, rather than moving the buttonhole over, which will throw off the center front. If necessary, redraw the neckline edge so that the neckline doesn't get lowered or redraw the bottom shaping. Don't forget to adjust the facing as well.

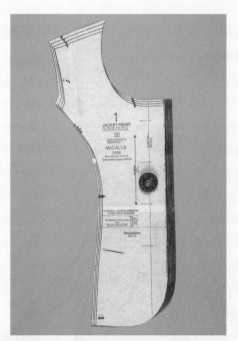

Oversize buttons need an extension on the front edge for the button to be centered properly.

9 Measure the front and back shoulders. If the front shoulder length is less than $\frac{1}{2}$ in. (1.3cm) smaller than the back, run an easeline on the back shoulder. If the front shoulder is more than $\frac{1}{2}$ in. (1.3cm) smaller, draw a 3-in. (7.6cm) long dart at the center of the back shoulder. Make the dart length the same width as the alteration amount, the difference between front and back.

Knock Knees

THE PROBLEM

Knock knees (knees that angle in) may go undetected in skirts, but cannot be hidden in pants, unless the pattern is adjusted. An array of fitting problems can crop up: pants hang off grain, wrinkles angle in toward the knee, and front crease lines angle inward. The pants get hung up on the knee, causing the pants leg to twist in whenever you sit or walk. In addition, the inner leg seam of the pants appears shorter near the hemline. This figure often has a flat spot under the hip which causes the pants to cave in at the side, causing still more wrinkles. The alterations given here solve this fitting problem by both lengthening the inner leg seam and shortening the side seam.

FAST FIT SOLUTION

Extend the grainline to the waist. Just below the crotch point, cut the pattern apart. Spread the pattern at the inner leg, and overlap it at the outer leg.

STEP-BY-STEP SOLUTION

1 Take a look at how much shorter your pants are in the inner leg. This will give you a hint at the alteration amount needed.

2 Draw a horizontal line across the front and back pattern pieces, 1 in. (2.5cm) under the crotch point.

3 Cut the pattern pieces completely apart along this line. Slide a piece of tissue paper under the two pieces.

4 Spread the pattern ¹/₂ in. to ³/₄ in. (1.3cm to 1.9cm) at the inner leg. Overlap the pattern ¹/₂ in. to ³/₄ in. (1.3cm to 1.9cm) on the outer leg, reducing the outer leg seamline length by ¹/₂ in. to ³/₄ in. (1.3cm to 1.9cm), the same amount the inner leg was spread. Repeat on the other pattern piece.

5 Tape to tissue paper. The seam lengths will match because the same alteration has been made on both the front and back legs (see "Checking the Grainline" on p. 193).

(see "Checking the Grainline" on p. 193).

> **FITTING TIP**
>
> Slightly fuller pants camouflage knock knees, allowing the pants to fall freely in a straight line from the crotch and hip. An overshirt that ends just above the knee also helps camouflage this problem.

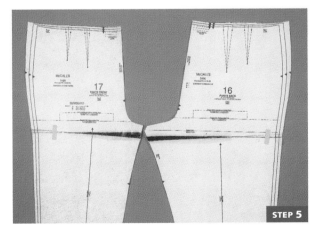

STEP 5

Knock knees need longer inner leg seams and shorter outer leg seams. Cut the pattern apart horizontally, and spread at the inner leg; overlap at the side seam.

PANTS FITTING THEORY

A quick glance in the mirror tells you your pants don't fit, but where to alter the pattern often remains a mystery. The first step to making pattern alterations is to identify the problems. When it comes to pants, most of us have more than one problem area. Start by examining the fit of your pants from every angle: Where are the wrinkles? Where are the side seams? How do the pants feel? By altering correctly and systematically, you can make great-looking pants that fit.

These are some typical symptoms and the fitting problems that they indicate:

• Wrinkles across the front thighs, resulting in "smiles" that radiate from the front crotch. The problem: full thighs.

• Diagonal wrinkles across the pants from hip to knee. The problem: high hip.

• Crotch feels too high, or too low. The problem: crotch length.

• Horizontal wrinkles radiate from the crotch in back. The problem: (1) a protruding seat or full thighs or (2) overfitting in the back.

• Pants pull too far down in the back when you sit. The problem: (1) not enough length on the back crotch hook and (2) possibly, not enough height on the waistline above the center back.

• Wrinkles under the back waistband. The problem: waistline slopes down in back.

• Your belly button is visible. The problem: not enough length on the pants front to cover the tummy.

• Side seams swing forward. The problem: swayback.

• Side seams swing backward. The problem: posture and a full high hip.

• Pants get hung up on calves in back. The problem: not enough pants width in the calf area.

• Diagonal wrinkles point from the crotch to the knee and just above in back. The problem: knock knees.

• Pants wrinkle under the seat in back. The problem: a flat seat or low derriere.

• Wrinkles point outward from the crotch toward the knee or pants hang off grain. The problem: bowed legs.

Bowed Legs

THE PROBLEM

Bowed legs can be hidden under a long skirt, but may become quite noticeable in pants. Contrary to what you might think, the space between the knees isn't the biggest clue. What's more noticeable is that the pants hang off grain, with wrinkles pointing outward toward the knee and the front crease line angling toward the outside of the leg. The solution is to add more length on the outer seam and subtract length on the inner leg seam.

FAST FIT SOLUTION

Extend the grainline to the waist. Just below the crotch point on front and back legs, cut the pattern apart horizontally. Spread the pattern at the outer leg and overlap it at the inner leg. To keep the pants on grain, use the grainline from the crotch up as reference when cutting out.

STEP-BY-STEP SOLUTION

1 Before you begin, extend the grainline to the waist on the front and back pattern pieces. After the pattern is altered, the new grainline will be from the crotch to the waist.

2 Draw a horizontal line across the front and back pattern pieces, 1 in. (2.5cm) below the crotch point. Cut the pattern completely apart along this line.

3 Slide a piece of tissue paper under the pattern pieces. Spread the pattern ½ in. to ¾ in. (1.3cm to 1.9cm) on the outer leg. Overlap the pattern ½ in. to ¾ in. (1.3cm to 1.9cm) on the inner leg, reducing the length of the inner leg seam ½ in. to ¾ in. (1.3cm to 1.9cm), the same amount you spread the outer leg. Repeat on the other pattern piece.

4 Tape the pattern pieces to tissue paper at the spread. Smooth out the inside and outside cutting lines so they blend into the originals. The seam lengths will match as you sew the front and back legs together.

> **FITTING FACT**
>
> Bow legs are camouflaged better by wearing slightly fuller pants in drapey fabric. The pants then hang from the hip and the inner leg, straightening out the curves.

STEP 4

Bowed legs need longer side seams and shorter inner leg seams. Cut the pattern apart horizontally and spread at the side seam; overlap at the inner leg seam.

CHECKING THE GRAINLINE

While the grainline is important on every garment, on pants it is even more so. Pants that hang on the grain do not stretch out of shape; this also prevents the legs from twisting. Multiple pants alterations can distort the grainline to the point that it may need to be re-established. An indication of distortion is if the grainline below your alteration slants. If this is the case, follow the steps below to re-establish the grainline.

1 On front and back pants pieces, start at the crotch point and draw a horizontal line across the pattern to intersect with the side seams.

2 Measure between the seamlines from the crotch point to the side seam on both front and back pieces separately. Then at the halfway point, mark an X on the pattern.

3 On the back piece only, move the X 1 in. (2.5cm) toward the side seam on the horizontal line.

4 Through the X on the front and back pieces, draw a vertical line from the waistline to the bottom of the pants, with the ruler perpendicular to the horizontal line. This is your new grainline.

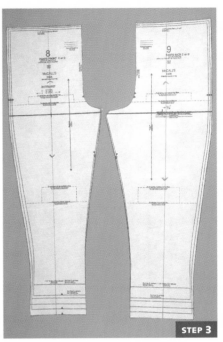

STEP 3

Alterations on pants can sometimes require correcting a distorted grainline.

Rising Front Waistline

THE PROBLEM

One of the hardest and most critical areas to fit on pants or a skirt is directly below the waistband. As women age, the waistline is no longer perpendicular to the floor. The front waistline arches up as the tummy gets bigger, bringing the pants or skirt front up with it. As a result, the front is shorter and may stick out at an angle. It's inevitable that most of us will put on a few pounds and inches over the years, so the alteration techniques in the next few sections will come in handy when altering for added girth around the stomach area. In this particular situation, it's tempting to widen the high hips and then take deeper darts for a snug fit at the waist—don't do it! Run an easeline instead. An overfitted garment molds to the tummy, thereby emphasizing the roundness. As a result, wrinkles form under the waistband and the hem is uneven because the tummy also lifts up the front of the garment. Instead, use a subtle alteration to prevent the side seams from pulling forward and the front hemline from poking out.

FAST FIT SOLUTION

Add extra fabric above the center front waist-line and width in the high hip and waist areas to release some of the stress across the tummy. Ease the excess width into a waistband that fits comfortably.

STEP-BY-STEP SOLUTION

1 Try on a finished skirt or pants from your closet that has this problem. Push down the waist at center front until the skirt hemline is even across the front or until the front crotch on pants doesn't pull up. There's a good chance that $\frac{1}{4}$ in. to $\frac{1}{2}$ in. (6mm to 1.3cm) will do the trick. If you've pushed the waist even farther—1 in. (2.5cm) or more—that's quite all right because your waistline may rise at center front. Whatever the amount, this is the size of your alteration.

FITTING TIP
To alter a pattern with side fronts, overlap the pattern pieces at the seamlines so that you can re-draw the waist cutting edge all the way across the front waist.

STEP 1

By pushing down the waist in center front you can see approximately how much you need to add for the front to hang well.

STEP 4

For a two-piece front, overlap the seamlines to redraw the waistline, giving height at center front. You may also need to add to the high hip and waist to give more room to the tummy.

2 Tape a piece of pattern paper above the waist on your skirt or pants front pattern piece. Temporarily tape the darts and pleats closed. Mark the alteration amount above the pattern's cutting line at center front.

3 Using a curved ruler, draw a new cutting line that arcs from the center front, tapering down to the original cutting line at the side seam. Untape the darts and pleats, then cut out the pattern piece.

4 If a horizontal wrinkle forms just under the waistband, you need to add width in the high hip and waist areas to release the stress across the tummy and to prevent the garment from getting hung up in these areas. To do this, add to the front and back side seams, smoothly tapering back to the original cutting line.

FITTING TIP

Not all patterns are created equal. If your waist and tummy are no longer small, Today's Fit pants patterns (in Vogue and Butterick) will need less adjustment.

STEP 6

·Within the seam allowance, run an easeline along the waist. Lock the ease in place by stabilizing the stitching with twill tape.

A FITTED WAISTBAND

If you're using the waistband that comes with the pants pattern and you need to let out the waist, you may not have enough fabric to cut a longer waistband. If you do a lot of pattern alterations, it is easier to cut a waistband that is long enough to accommodate alterations and style options. To cover all waist options, including fly fronts, pocket openings, and zippered openings, cut the waistband length to your honest waist measurement plus 6 in. (15.2cm). For a waistband that is 1¼ in. (4.4cm) wide, cut the waistband 4 in. (10.2cm) wide. For a 1-in. (2.5cm)

band, cut the waistband 3⅜ in. (8.6cm) wide. Whenever possible, cut one long side on a selvege.

Notch the waistband 1 in. (2.5cm) from one end, this will be the clean finish end, ending evenly with the garment. From this notch, measure toward the opposite end, your waist measurement plus ½ in. (1.3cm). Tooth to tooth around the circumference of a skirt or pants, the garment fits into the notched area on the waistband. The extra fabric on this end can be used for underlap or other style treatments. The beauty of this waistband is that it always fits.

5 Cut out your garment pieces, sew the waistline darts or pleats, and add pockets. The pattern addition at the side seam makes your garment larger than the waistband, so you need to draw it in with ease. Don't dart out the added fabric.

6 Using a 3mm stitch length, sew two ease-lines near (or on top of) each other ½ in. (1.3cm) from the waist cutting line. To lock the easelines in, sew or press on a ¼-in. (6mm) wide length of twill tape on top of the ease stitching. Sew the side seam.

> **FITTING TIP**
>
> By updating your body measurements every year, you can make alterations to improve the fit of your clothes, making it less obvious if you've gained weight.

MAKE UP A PANTS PRETEST

The best way to begin the pants-fitting process is by making a pretest. Not only will you get the perfect pair of pants the first time around, but you'll also understand what kinds of alterations to do on future garments. Follow these instructions to make up a pants pretest.

1 Outline your size or sizes on the pattern with a highlighter pen.

2 Adjust the crotch length. Refer to your crotch length measurement and compare it to a favorite pair of pants you own (see "Duplicating Pants You Love" on p. 220). The difference is the crotch length adjustment. On a pair of fitted trousers, the crotch should ride ½ in. (1.3cm) from the body; on a trouser, ¾ in. (1.9cm); and on full pants, 1½ in. (3.8cm). Any more or less indicates that the crotch length needs to be adjusted.

3 Adjust the pants length by comparing your own pants length measurement or the length of your favorite pair of pants with the finished length given on the back of the pattern envelope. To maintain the integrity of the style, lengthen both above and below the knee, not just at the pants bottom (see "Altering Length" on p. 71). Smooth out the jogs on the inner and outer leg caused by shortening.

4 Cut a pair of pants from scrap fabric with an additional 1 in. (2.5cm) at the side seams, inner leg seams, and above the waistline.

5 With tracing paper, mark the highlighted seamlines at the side and optional seamlines at the inner legs, as determined by your desired pattern adjustments. This will give you a point of reference when you make alterations.

6 Run an easeline on the waist seamline. Stabilize with twill tape.

7 Construct the scrap-fabric pants, trying different combinations at the inner leg until any fitting problems over the thigh or backside are corrected.

8 Refine the fit and transfer all findings to a master pattern.

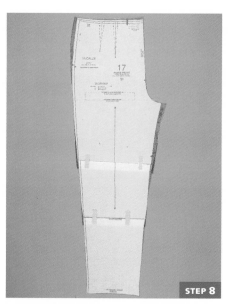

STEP 8

After altering your pants pattern to the perfect shape, stabilize it by pressing onto a fusible interfacing.

Big Tummy, Skinny Legs

THE PROBLEM

If you have a rather large tummy and thin legs, the circumference of the leg is often too wide, especially if you are short. In this case, altering a pants pattern at the side seam is not always the answer, because you can't take in the legs enough. Since most of your fullness is in the tummy, why not add to the pattern exactly where you need it—in the tummy area only? The following alteration will increase the girth in the tummy without increasing the size of the legs. This will also allow the pleats to stay closed, which improves the appearance of the garment.

FAST FIT SOLUTION

Measure the waist, full hip, and tummy areas on yourself and the pattern to determine how much needs to be added. Cut the pattern vertically from the waist to within $1/4$ in. (6mm) of the pants bottom, and spread the pattern as needed in the tummy area. Reposition darts or pleats, and check the grainline to avoid distortion.

STEP-BY-STEP SOLUTION

1 Take an up-to-date set of body measurements for the waist, full hip, and the all-important tummy measurement 3 in. (7.6cm) down from the waistline, adding 1 in. to

1½ in. (2.5cm to 3.8cm) for ease. The tummy measurement plus ease equals the total amount you need in this area.

FITTING TIP

If your tummy is large and your legs are either small or short, use a size smaller pattern on the lower leg (if you have a multisize pattern). Make smooth transitions to the smaller size, starting at the end of your fullest spot.

2 On the front pants pattern, fold out front pleats all the way to the crotch. If the pattern has no pleats, pin out darts in the back and front.

3 If the pants have slant pocket styling, pin the side front in place, matching the sewing line on the front to the pocket placement line on the side front. Slide the side front behind the front, matching the dots.

4 On the front pattern piece, measure 3 in. (7.6cm) down the side seam from the waistline. At this point, place the ruler perpendicular to the grainline and draw a line across the pattern in the tummy area. The line will not be quite 3 in. (7.6cm) down at the center front. This simulates the measurement on the body, because the distance is naturally shorter from the waistline at the center front than it is from the waist at the sides.

5 Measure across the pattern from center front to side seam. Do not include seam allowances or the zipper placket allowance. This measurement is the amount you'll have when the pants are complete with the pocket, pleats, and zipper.

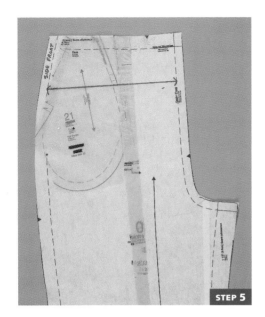

STEP 5

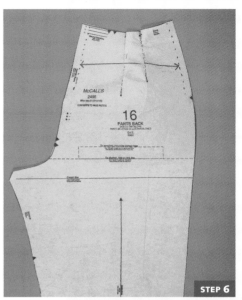

STEP 6

With pleats and darts folded out and the side front pinned into position, take a flat pattern measure across the front, 3 in. (7.6cm) down from the waistline, from center front to side seam (left). Measure the back pattern piece the same way (right).

6 Measure the back pattern piece in the same manner, from side seam to center back. Fold out any darts for the measurement.

7 Add the front and back measurements together and multiply times two, since each front and back pattern piece represents only half of the pants. Compare the pattern measurement to your actual tummy measurement, including ease. The difference between the two is the amount you need to add for the pants to fit comfortably and be flattering over the tummy.

8 Decide where to add the additional fabric. If your body is round both front and back, and you have some fullness on the back high hip as well as the tummy, divide by four and add at both front and back side seams, taper-

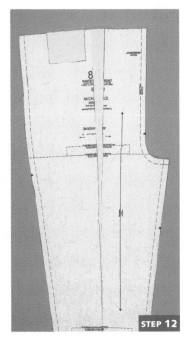

STEP 12

To get extra room over the tummy, spread the pants front. Cut out the pleat box for repositioning later.

ing back to the original cutting line by the full hip. If all or most of your fullness is concentrated in the tummy, add it all right where you need it—on the front, in the tummy area. If a total addition of 3 in. (7.6cm) or less is needed, add half of your total amount to each pants front. If your measurements indicate an addition of more than 3 in. (7.6cm), add some to the front and some to the back. The amounts added do not have to be equal on front and back.

9 Leaving the grainline intact, draw a line from the waistline of the pants to the bottom edge of the pants parallel to the grainline, near the original position of the pleat or dart closest to the center front.

10 Cut out the section involving the darts or pleats on the front and save it to reposition later. Put aside the side front if the pattern has one.

11 Cut the pattern open along this vertical line from the waist to within $1/4$ in. (6mm) of the bottom edge of the pants. Slide a piece of paper under the pattern tissue.

12 Spread the top of the pants open until you have the desired amount needed between the opening in the tummy area. The addition tapers to zero by the bottom of the pants or sooner. The waistline seems to slant up after this alteration, which means you may not need extra length to go over the tummy.

> **FITTING TIP**
> Creases in pants are much easier to press if they are pressed in before the pants are put together. Fusible thread in the bobbin gives a sharp crease when pressed.

13 To position the styling elements proportionally, reposition pleats or darts so that half the amount of the addition is on either side of the spread or one side of the pleat is in line with the crease line (see "Crease Line Positioning" below).

14 Check to make sure that the grainline has not been distorted after this alteration (see "Checking the Grainline" on p. 193).

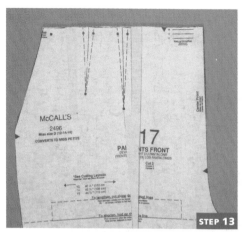

After spreading the front of the pattern, reposition darts or pleats so that half the addition is on either side or one side of the pleat is in line with one crease line.

CREASE LINE POSITIONING

For clean-looking pleats that hang well, position the pleats in line with the front crease line on pants, rather than toward the side seam on center front. To find the crease line, line up the inner and outer leg cutting lines from the knee to the bottom of the pants. From the knee up let the pattern stay on grain; the center and side seamlines will not match from the knee up. Front creases extend to the waistline and back creases to the crotch line. Once you determine the front crease line, you can reposition a pleat so the edge closest to the center front is right on the crease.

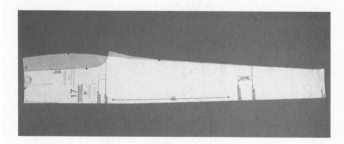

To find the crease line on pants, line up the inner and outer leg cutting lines from the knee to the bottom of the pants. From the knee up, let the pattern stay on grain.

FRONT STAY FLATTENS TUMMY

A pants front stay helps flatten the tummy and keep pleats and pockets from opening, no matter how much you eat. A pants front stay is merely an extension of the side front pattern piece, which is extended from the front edge of the pocket so that it can be included in the center front seam.

1 Fold out any pleats and or darts on the front pants piece, folding the pleats all the way out to the crotch.

2 Tape a 6-in. (15.2cm) wide paper extension to the rounded side of the side front piece, which is opposite the side seam.

3 Slide the side front piece with the paper extension under the front pants piece with the pleats and darts folded out, matching up the placement dots at the top and bottom of the pants pieces.

4 On the paper extension, trace the top waistline edge and center front edge of pocket piece.

5 Remove the pants front piece from the side front. Make a mark 5 in. (12.7cm) down from the waistline on the center front. Connect this mark to the bottom of the pocket, blending into a smooth, curved line.

6 After the center front seam is sewn through the pants and through the pants front stay, the seam allowance on the front stay can be reduced to ½ in. (1.3cm) to eliminate seam bulk.

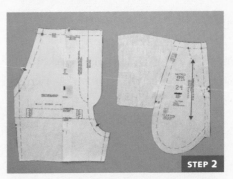

Fold out front pleats to crotch. Add paper extension to rounded side of side front, above pocket bag.

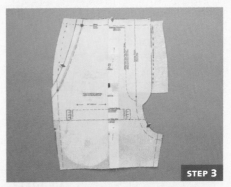

Slide side front behind front, matching placement dots.

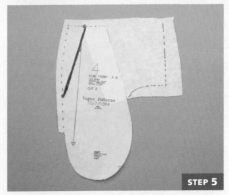

Front stay is 5 in. (12.7cm) long at center front and blends to rounded edge of side front pocket bag.

Tight across the Middle

THE PROBLEM

When waistlines are tight and fabric rides up over the tummy, the culprit is twofold: You are not being honest about your waist measurement, and you are not allowing enough room over the tummy and high hip area. You may think that a smaller waist on garments makes you look smaller, but in fact, a tight waistband makes you look bigger, because everything bulges out above and below it. In addition, a tight waistband is uncomfortable—buttons and hooks pop off and the waistband wrinkles. It's time to remeasure your waist…and be honest!

FAST FIT SOLUTION

Take an accurate measurement of your waist and cut a longer waistband, including extra amounts for darts and pleats, finishing the ends. Compare your waistline measurement to that of the pattern; add extra fabric at the side seams to accommodate your high hip and tummy. Ease the additional fabric into the new waistband.

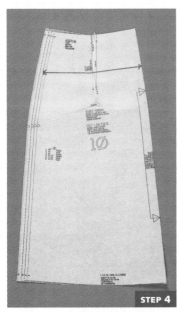

STEP 4

Fold out darts and pleats; then measure between the seamlines, 3 in. (7.6cm) below the waistline seam.

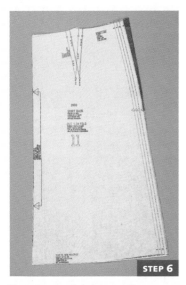

STEP 6

To get extra fabric over the tummy, you must make an addition at the side seam that goes into the waist. This will be eased in to fit the waistline.

STEP-BY-STEP SOLUTION

1 Measure your waist. Add 1 in. (2.5cm) to allow for the bulk of darts and seams. Your pants or skirt must now fit into a waistband that is 1 in. (2.5cm) larger than your waist.

2 Cut a waistband that is 4 in. (10.2cm) longer than your waist measurement and $3^3/_8$ in. (8.6cm) wide. Notch the band $1^1/_2$ in. (3.8cm) from each end. This length gives you your waist plus 1 in. (2.5cm), and plenty of fabric on each end for finishing the ends.

3 Fold out all darts and pleats on the pattern.

4 Measure the skirt or pants at the high hip, between the seamlines. For the garment to fit smoothly over a body that has a tummy and some high-hip fullness, it should measure 3 in. (7.6cm) larger than your high hip measurement. If it doesn't, add the extra amount necessary at the side seams.

5 Compare your high hip plus 3 in. (7.6cm) of ease to the flat pattern measurement. The difference is the total alteration amount. Divide by four; this is the alteration amount at the side seams. A typical addition is $1/_4$ in. to $1/_2$ in. (6mm to 1.3cm).

6 Make the addition to the side seams at the waistline, tapering the addition to zero 7 in. (17.8cm) down the hip. This will give you the additional fabric you need over the high hip and tummy.

7 Sew all darts and pleats in the garment. Run an easeline ³⁄₈ in. to ¹⁄₂ in. (1cm to 1.3cm) from the cut edge of the waist on the garment. You can ease in ¹⁄₈ in. per inch (3mm per 2.5cm) of fabric without residual puckers after it is pressed. If the fabric is heavy, lengthen your stitch. You can run an additional easeline over the first if you need to.

8 Remeasure the waist on all pieces between seamlines to make sure you have eased in enough. It should measure your waist measurement plus ¹⁄₂ in. to 1 in. (6mm to 2.5cm) for ease, taken up by the bulk of the waistband.

9 When the measurement is correct, stabilize the ease by pressing or sewing over the easeline with narrow, ¹⁄₄-in. (6mm), twill tap, or a strip of narrow, straight-grain fusible tape. This step is a must, or the ease will slip away as you sew on the waistband.

Run an easeline within the seam allowance at the waist.

Lock the easeline in place by stabilizing with twill tape.

STRAIGHT SKIRTS

If your figure is not what it used to be, fear not—your straight skirt days aren't over. The right kind of straight skirt can be flattering on just about any type of figure. As I've explained in other below-the-waist alterations, fit is all about camouflage. If you love straight skirts but think they won't look good on you, try Vogue 7333. It's truly the most forgiving straight skirt I've ever worn. It doesn't cup under the tummy, and the size of the waist is realistic, giving more room for comfort and camouflage. It also gets slimmer at the hemline for a very flattering silhouette.

High Hip

THE PROBLEM

Anyone who has a high hip is likely well aware of it. A high hip (when one hip is higher than the other) causes diagonal wrinkles to form across the front and back, originating at the high hip and angling toward the opposite knee. In addition, seamlines won't hang straight as the high hip forces garments to hang off grain. As a result, the seat and knees become stretched out of shape. By altering the pattern before you cut, all of these problems disappear.

FAST FIT SOLUTION

Determine the alteration amount needed to accommodate the high hip. On both front and back pieces of the high hip side, cut the pattern horizontally from center front to side, just under the waist. Spread the pattern as necessary at the side.

STEP-BY-STEP SOLUTION

1 Determine how much higher one hip is than the other. To do this, put a narrow belt or a 1-in. (2.5cm) wide piece of elastic around your waist, and take off your shoes. Slip a large paper clip into the hole on the

end of a tape measure. Step on the paper clip and position the tape measure along your left side. Measure up the side of your left leg from the floor to the bottom of the elastic or belt. Take the same measurement on your right side.

2 Compare left and right measurements. The difference is the amount by which you will have to adjust the high side on your pattern.

3 Make a copy of your back and front pants or skirt piece. Label all pieces: "left front," "right front," "left back," and "right back."

4 On the high side, draw a horizontal line across the pattern from center front to the side about 1 in. (2.5cm) from the waistline. Cut the pattern along this line, leaving the pattern intact for ½ in. (1.3cm) near center front.

5 Place tissue paper under the pattern. Lift the upper section of the cut pattern near the waist so that the upper and lower portion of the skirt or pants spreads the high hip amount. Alter both front and back pieces in this manner on the high side.

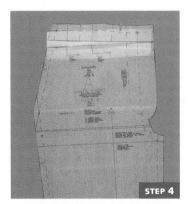

STEP 4

Cut the pattern apart horizontally 1 in. down from the waistline and lift the upper section near the waist.

FITTING TIP

If your high hip is less than ⅜ in. (1cm) higher than your other hip, cut fronts and backs double with 1-in. (2.5cm) seam allowances at the waistline and side seams. Sew the seams at ⅝ in. (1.5cm) on the high side, and 1 in. (2.5cm) on the other side; the two amounts will blend together at center front and center back.

HIGH HIP ALTERATIONS
FOR A DRESS, COAT, OR JACKET

A high hip may not be as noticeable in loose-fitting dresses, coats, or jackets without a waist-line seam, but it's still possible that a diagonal wrinkle from high hip to knee will develop. The following alteration will help adjust these types of garments to account for a high hip.

1 Since you'll be cutting the left and right sides separately, make a copy of the pattern pieces and label the copies "left" and "right."

2 Make alterations on the original pattern pieces for both front and back on the high hip side. Draw a horizontal line across the pattern, 1 in. (2.5cm) above the waistline.

3 Starting at the side seam, cut across this line to the center front; if it is princess style, cut to the side front. Leave the pattern intact at the edge opposite the side seam so that it can act as a hinge.

4 Lift the top half of the pattern, creating an opening between the top and bottom of the pattern that is equal to the total amount of your high hip alteration.

5 At the side seam, add half the amount of the high hip alteration that was made above the waistline.

6 Smooth out the waistline curve at the side seam so it is curved in a bit at the waist, similar to the unaltered side.

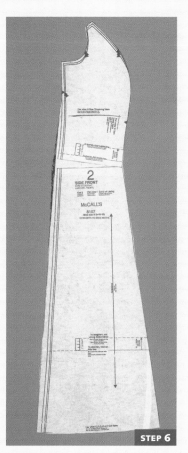

STEP 6

The top half of this one-piece dress pattern has been lifted at the side seam, tapering to the original by the side front. The side seam waistline was redrawn so that it curves in nicely at the waist.

HIGH HIP AND POCKETS

If you've tried to adjust for a high hip in the past, you may have avoided pockets because you weren't sure how to alter them. In reality, no adjustment is necessary on either the side front or the pocket facing. The pocket moves up and down as you adjust for the amount of the high hip. Try the following and you'll be convinced.

1 Make a copy of your front and back pattern pieces, because you'll need to cut the right and left sides separately if one hip is higher by more than ⅜ in. (1cm). Label the copy "left" or "right." Make alterations on the original pattern pieces, which can be kept as a reference for future adjustments.

2 Cut the pattern apart ½ in. to 1 in. (1.3cm to 2.5cm) from the side seam. If a seam allowance is marked on your pattern, use it as a cutting line.

3 Position a large piece of tissue paper under the front and back pattern pieces near the side seam, extending across the waistline. On both front and back, add half of the high hip adjustment along the side seam, tapering to zero by the knee.

4 Above the waistline at the side seam, add the total amount of the high hip adjustment. Taper the addition along the waistline to zero by the center front and center back. Add a bit of length at the bottom side seam where the section was lifted.

5 Now for the pocket test: Overlay the side front onto the front, matching the pattern marking for the dots and squares. A miracle—it fits! No alterations are needed on the side front, and thus no alterations are needed on the pocket facing.

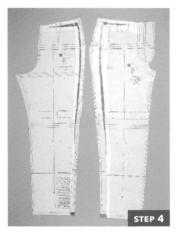

STEP 4

For a high hip adjustment, add at the side seam and lift at the waistline.

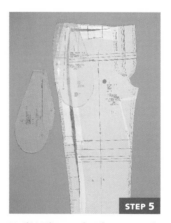

STEP 5

Voilà! The pocket has moved with the adjustment, so no addition is needed on side front or pocket facing.

Full Hips

THE PROBLEM

You've finally gotten a garment to fit in the hip, but now the waist is too large—is this an indication of full hips? You might think so, but it could be one of two things: large hips or a small waist. A quick look in the mirror will tell the story.

If your hips are large in proportion to the upper part of your body, then full hips are the problem. If your hips are in proportion to the upper part of the body, but the waist appears small, then the problem lies in your waist. If your waist is small, the garment's waist can be reduced by increasing the width of darts and pleats. If your hips are large, the pattern needs to be increased at the side seam in the hip area.

The biggest mistake a full-hipped individual makes is thinking that pants that are snug in the hips will hold in the hips, making them look smaller. This is not so! To camouflage a full hip, the garment actually needs to be looser so it won't lock onto the fullness. Full hips are better in drapey fabric, in styles that are fuller at the hem, so that the hip appears smaller by comparison. For the alteration given here, you will need to know your full hip measurement, and how far down it is from your waist (see "Personal Measurement Chart" on p. 9).

FAST FIT SOLUTION

Determine the alteration amount by comparing your full hip measurement plus ease to that of the pattern measurement. Make an addition to each side seam at the hip, tapering out half of the addition by the bottom of the garment. A large addition may also require adding at the waist, so that the side seams will not wrinkle when pressed open.

STEP-BY-STEP SOLUTION

1 Measure the circumference of your full hip, and the distance it is from your waist.

2 On the pattern, measure down the side seam the distance of your full hip, starting at the waistline seam. Mark this spot with an X. Then highlight the sizes that fit your measurements with a highlighter pen, making smooth transitions to the smaller size at the waist.

3 At the spot marked with an X, draw a line across the pattern perpendicular to the grainline.

4 On this line, measure between the seamlines of your size on the front and back of your pattern. Compare the flat pattern measurement to your measurement plus ease. The

> **FITTING TIP**
> The circumference at the bottom of a straight skirt or full pants can always be tapered in for a slimmer effect. But don't overdo it—too much tapering leaves the hips looking larger.

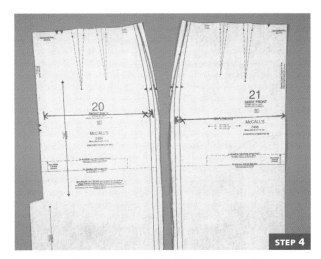

STEP 4

Measuring the pattern at the full hip is your only insurance of a flattering fit. Measure between the seamlines but not into the seam allowance.

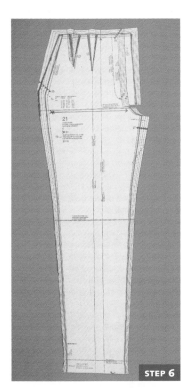

STEP 6

If you have to add a great deal at the hip, you will need to add some at the waist so that the curve at the side seam is not too pronounced. The waist can be reduced by increasing the size of the darts and the pleats.

difference is the total alteration amount. Divide this by four to determine the amount you need to add to each side seam at the hip.

5 Make the side seam addition. Taper in only half of the addition by the bottom of the garment; tapering in the full addition will just emphasize the problem.

6 If you're adding a lot—more than ¹/₂ in. (1.3cm)—at each side seam, you'll also need to add to the waist. The extra at the waist can be taken out with wider darts or pleats (see "Small Waist" on the facing page). Make a gradual transition into the waist for a flattering silhouette; a curve that is too steep wrinkles when sewn in fabric and put on the body.

Small Waist

THE PROBLEM

At first glance, a small waist is often misunderstood as full hips. But if you first referred to the full hips alteration (p. 212) and discovered that you have a small waist instead, then consider yourself lucky. Unfortunately, however, it's likely that the waist on everything you buy is always too big.

The most obvious solution, but not always the best, is to take in the waist at the side seam. If you don't need to take in more than $\frac{1}{2}$ in. (1.3cm) on each side seam—for a total of 2 in. (5cm)—this method will work. But if you are using a multisize pattern and the change is more than two sizes between the hip and the waist, you'll wind up making your hips look too large. Better results come from taking in all of the styling elements. Small changes in many places yield more flattering results. What works best for the small waist is increasing the width of styling elements and taking in at the side seam.

FAST FIT SOLUTION

Determine the alteration amount by comparing your waist measurement to that of the pattern. If the amount is less than 2 in. (5cm), simply take it in at the side seams. If it is more, take in at the side seams and increase the size of all styling elements.

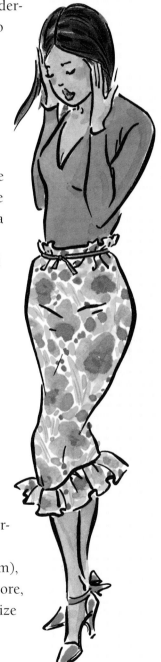

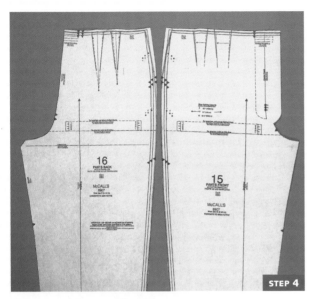

One way to decrease the size of the waist is by increasing the width of all the styling elements.

STEP 4

STEP-BY-STEP SOLUTION

1 Decide how much to reduce the waist by comparing your waist measurement to the waist measurement on the size you will be using. If the change is no more than two sizes smaller than the hip, simply take it in at the side seams. Otherwise, you'll also have to increase the size of the styling elements.

2 Add up the number of styling elements available. For example, if your pants pattern has two front pleats and two back darts, a total of eight styling elements can be increased in size (since you'll be cutting the pattern double).

3 Divide the number of styling elements into the amount you want to reduce the waist. For example, if you want to reduce the waist by 4 in. (10.2cm) and you have eight styling elements, increase the size of each styling element by ¼ in. (6mm) or ⅛ in. (3mm) on each side. Then take out the other 2 in. (5cm) by reducing the waist at the side seam ½ in. (1.3cm)

4 Sew the side of each pleat and dart deeper by ⅛ in. (3mm) on each side. Taper the increase gradually, just before the high hip if your fullness starts early.

FITTING TIP

If your hip curve is flat just under the high hip area, reverse the convex curve on front and back to make a more concave curve, reflecting your body. This is better done in the fitting; but after a few times, you will recognize when the hip curve is too full and be able to flatten it out while sewing.

Large Waist

THE PROBLEM

For many of us, as we increase in years our waistline also increases at a steady rate. (They say it's a natural sign of aging!) Too-tight waistlines are not only uncomfortable but also unflattering. The waistbands crinkle, buttons and hooks pop off, and you may even need to unbutton your skirt or pants to sit down.

Adding at the side seam increases the size of the waist. Another option is to eliminate or decrease the size of any darts. The purpose of a dart is to give shape to a garment, to take away fullness where we don't need it and give us fullness where we do. In the case of a large waist, darts should be smaller, fewer, or even eliminated altogether. Instead, replacing the darts with an easeline over the tummy can be more flattering.

Many women with a large waist also have a full high hip and a large tummy, fitting problems that can be fixed with other alterations (see pp. 212 and 177). Alterations for these problems may solve the large waist problem as well. If you have either a full high hip or a large tummy, try those alterations first.

FAST FIT SOLUTION

Decrease the size of darts. Add to the side seam at the waist and high hip, tapering back to the original cutting line by the side seam.

STEP-BY-STEP SOLUTION

1 If the pattern is multisize, cut a size larger at the waist. This may give you the waist size you need. If not, proceed with Steps 2 to 4.

2 Add up the number of darts on the garment. If your front and back pattern pieces both have two darts, you have a total of eight styling elements that can be adjusted, because

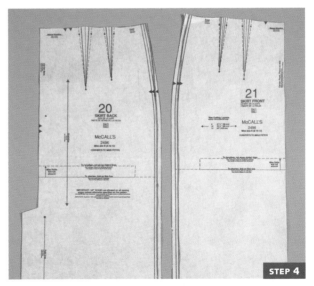

Larger waists need smaller or fewer darts, and no more than a ½-in. (1.3cm) addition at the side.

you will be cutting the pattern pieces double. If you sew each side of every dart $\frac{1}{8}$ in. (3mm) smaller, you have increased your waist by 2 in. (5cm). Redraw new sewing lines on the darts.

3 Subtract the amount you will gain by letting out the darts from the total amount you need. Divide the remainder by four; this is the correct amount to add to each of the side seams at the waist.

4 Slide extra pattern tissue under the side seams, and make the addition. Using a curved ruler, taper out the addition by the full hip. Avoid completely eliminating the curve at the side seam, or the garment will appear shapeless. If you're adding more than $\frac{1}{2}$ in. (1.3cm) on each side of the waist, do not taper to the original at the side seam; instead, taper to half the alteration at the hip and add half of the alteration at the hip even if you don't need it. This results in more flattering proportions.

5 An alternative is to eliminate some of the darts. If the front or back has four darts, two can be eliminated. Simply move the remaining one over so that its new position is in the middle of the two original darts.

> **FITTING TIP**
>
> If you want your pants leg narrower at the bottom, taper the inner and outer legs the same amount on the front and back, finishing the taper by the crotch line or 5 in. (12.7cm) above the knee if your calves are full.

DUPLICATING PANTS YOU LOVE

Most of us have a pair of favorite pants in our wardrobe that feel great and have a flattering fit. But chances are it was difficult to find them at all, and it will probably be even more difficult to find another pair. So why not sew the perfect pair of pants yourself? It's easier than you think to re-create the fit of a pair of ready-to-wear pants you love. As you peruse pattern books, look for a style similar to your favorite pair. In other words, if your favorite pair of pants has pleats, then don't choose a pants pattern with a flat front and darts.

1 Start by measuring the width of the leg bottom of your favorite pants. You can do this easily by doubling the measurement of the bottom of the pants as they lie flat on the table.

2 Next, measure the width of the thighs, at the crotch point and the knee. Look for a pants pattern with a similar pants leg circumference (listed on the back of the pattern envelope) as your favorite. It's easy

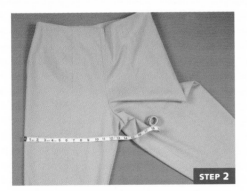

Measure your favorite pants at the thigh and knee.

Look for a pattern with a similar leg circumference (listed on the back of the pattern envelope) as your favorite pants.

to change pants circumference by 2 in. (5cm) or less, but more than that is a bit tricky; look for another pattern instead.

3 Turn your favorite pair of pants wrong side out. Slide one leg inside the other so that the crotch curve is clearly visible. Measure the back crotch to the bottom of the waistband or, if there is no waistband, to the waistline seam. Measure the front and back crotch separately.

4 Try on your favorite pair of pants again and study them critically, especially in the crotch length area. Is there anything you want changed? Add or subtract crotch length changes to the measurements taken in Step 3.

5 Using a highlighter pen, outline your size on the pattern according to your measurements. If your waist corresponds

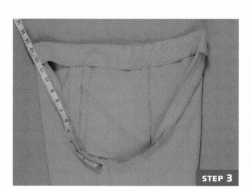

Measure the front and back crotch curves from the bottom of the waistband to the crotch point at inner leg.

to a size 14 but your hip measurement indicates a size 12, smoothly grade from the size 14 cutting line at the waist to the size 12 cutting line at the hip. Multisize patterns make this alteration a snap.

6 Measure the front and back crotch curves of the pattern pieces separately by putting the tape measure on its side and measuring from the waistline to the cutting point. Lengthen or shorten between the crotch and the waist only by the smaller amount, or the amount that is common to both front and back. Read about altering pants on p. 229 before making further adjustments.

7 Fold up the hem allowance on the pattern; it is easier to evaluate length on a pretest pair without a hem allowance. Cut out the pants with 1-in. (2.5cm) seam allowances at the side seams, inner leg, and above the waistline.

8 Make up a pretest pair of pants. Stabilize the waistline with twill tape before trying the garment on, then refine the fit, including the length.

9 Make alterations on the pattern. Stabilize the pattern against wear and tear by fusing it with a dry iron to a stabilizer.

On your pattern piece, measure front and back crotch curves separately between the seamlines.

DART KNOW-HOW

Darts play an important role in many garments, enhancing fit and adding attractive design lines. But before you use them, it's important to consider dart placement and dart construction for the best effect.

Dart legs can be straight or curved to conform to the shape of the body. On pants and skirt backs, dart legs can be curved in to give more fabric to a rounded high hip or curved out to take in fullness above a protruding seat. Both legs of the dart must be the same length, or the dart won't hang straight on the body; typically, front darts are 3½ in. (8.1cm) long.

The middle of a front dart is usually 3½ in. (8.1cm) from the center front. On skirts and pants, the middle of the second dart is 2¼ in. (5.6cm) over from the first, toward the side seam. Darts can always be repositioned, as long as they point to an area of fullness.

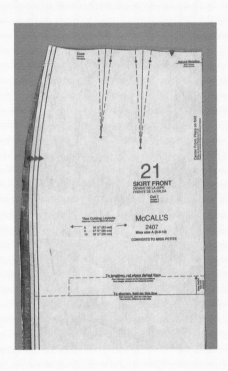

Flat Seat

THE PROBLEM

A flat seat is easily recognized by others, but it's not a view we usually have of ourselves (thank heavens)! If you look at your backside in the mirror and see wrinkles and overall bagginess under the crotch of your pants, it's a good indication that you have a flat seat. Vertical and horizontal wrinkles may also appear on the back of a skirt (but the front hangs nicely), or the back leg of your pants may not hang straight because the legs catch on well-developed calves. Fitting problems at the derriere are very common: your backside may be flat, protruding, high, low—or a combination of these.

Getting a good fit is a matter of proportion, rather than overall body measurements. Just as some people wear different sizes on top and bottom, some individuals are one or two sizes smaller in the back than in the front. The tummy may protrude in front, needing a wider front; and a seat flat enough that horizontal wrinkles are created indicates the need for a size reduction.

On a skirt, most women with a flat seat need few, if any, darts in the back. On a flat seat, back darts provide extra fabric fullness, resulting in horizontal wrinkles that draw attention to the flat seat. Also, the back of the skirt becomes smaller than the front. If you're dealing with pants, the question is how and where to get rid of the excess fabric. A flat seat

FITTING TIP

It's helpful to make a pretest pair of pants from scrap fabric to determine the right amount to reduce the back inner leg. If you take away too much, your body will steal fabric from the front crotch when you walk or sit, causing front crotch "smiles."

FITTING TIP

If you have well-developed calves or lock your knees when you stand, taper out to a larger size just above the knee. The excess fabric ensures that pants won't catch on the calves or knees.

needs less room in the back crotch, so it can be made shorter than usual. Reducing the length of the back inner leg seam is a simple way to pull in and give some shape to the back inner leg. A back inner leg seam length that is $1/2$ in. (1.3cm) shorter than the front inner leg seam length is a great way to pull in some of the fullness under the seat.

FAST FIT SOLUTION

If you have a flat seat there are several options: Option 1, cut a smaller size on the back inner leg, lower the center back waistline, and reduce the width of the back darts; option 2, reduce the length of the back inner leg seam; and, if the problem persists, option 3, split the back pants piece and overlap the tissue within.

STEP-BY-STEP SOLUTION

Option 1

1 Trace your size or sizes on the pattern with a highlighter pen. On the back leg inseam, use one or two sizes smaller from the crotch point to the knee. On a one-size pattern piece, move in the back leg inseam cutting line $1/2$ in. (1.3cm) from the crotch to the knee, tapering to the original cutting line from the knee to the hem. Trace the new cutting line on the pattern piece.

2 Decide if you need to lift the center back. Try lifting the center back on a pair of pants or skirt you own to see if they hang better. If it works, lower the back waistline (the equivalent to lifting the skirt on the body) at center back $1/2$ in. (1.3cm), tapering to zero by the side seam.

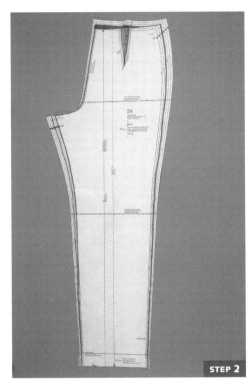

Cut the back inner leg two sizes smaller
to the knee. Lower the center back ½ in.
(2.5cm), and make back darts narrower.

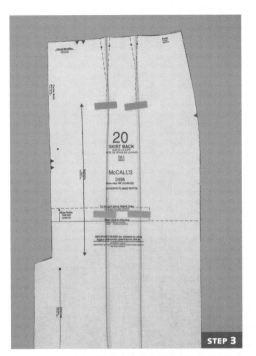

Flat seats need little
back darting. To make
the whole back smaller
on pants and skirts, fold
out half the size of a back
dart from waist to hem.

3 On skirts and pants, fold out half the size
of a back dart from waist to hem, or eliminate darts altogether if you have a large waist.

4 The waist can be taken in a bit to give
shape by running an easeline within
the seam allowance and stabilizing it with
twill tape.

Option 2

1 Measure the length of the front and back
inner leg seams on the pattern. If both
seams are the same length, make the following
adjustment to the back leg.

2 Just under the crotch, draw a horizontal line across the back pants piece, perpendicular to the grainline.

3 Cut the pattern apart from the crotch to the side seamline, leaving a hinge at the side seamline to hold the pattern together.

4 Overlap the pattern at the inner leg $1/4$ in. to $1/2$ in. (6mm to 1.3cm), so that the back inner leg seam length is a total of $1/2$ in. (1.3cm) shorter than the front. Taper the reduction to zero by the side seamline. Smooth out the inner leg seamline.

5 When sewing the inner leg seam, pin the seams together on a 1 to 1 ratio from the hem to the knee. From the knee to the crotch, let the feed dogs ease in the extra length on the front inner leg to the back. Sew with the back piece next to the presser foot and the front piece next to the feed dogs.

6 After the alteration is complete, check the grainline to make sure it hasn't become distorted (see "Checking the Grainline" on p. 193).

> **FITTING FACT**
>
> **Front and back crotch measurements differ greatly on larger women. The crotch length may be 4 in. to 6 in. (10.2cm to 15.2cm) longer in the back than in the front because of a full high hip or bottom and pants that are worn under the tummy in front.**

Option 3

1 Draw a horizontal line across the back leg, 3 in. (7.6cm) below the crotch.

2 Draw a vertical line in the middle of the back leg from top to bottom.

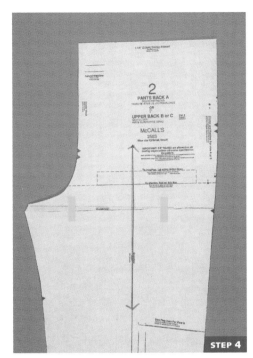

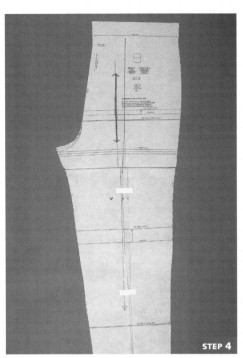

STEP 4

STEP 4

Option 2: To pull in some fullness in the crotch area, draw a horizontal line perpendicular to the grainline across the back pants piece, under the crotch. Cut the pattern apart almost to the side seam, and take out ½ in. (1.3cm). The back inner leg should never be more than ½ in. (1.3cm) shorter than the front inner leg.

Option 3: Split the pattern from waist to calf and across the crotch. Overlap ½ in. (1.3cm) just under the backside, reducing some of the fullness.

3 Cut the pattern apart along these lines, leaving ¼ in. (6mm) for a hinge at all outside edges.

4 Overlap the back leg vertically, taking out ½ in. to 1 in. (1.3cm to 2.5cm) total; taper the reduction to zero at the inner and outer leg cutting lines. Try not to reduce too much at the full hip. To help the pattern flatten, let it overlay slightly in the middle of the horizontal line.

Low Seat

THE PROBLEM

A friend of mine swore she heard her derriere drop on her 30th birthday. While she was certainly exaggerating, her biological clock was right on time. If you have a low backside, you'll notice that it tends to push down the crotch of your pants, resulting in wrinkles that radiate out from the last few inches of the derriere. The waist also pulls down at center back because of the seat's low position. Whether your backside is flat, protruding, or normal, it can also be low. A sideways glance in the mirror will tell the story. However, a low seat often seems to go hand-in-hand with a flat one. (For instructions on altering for a flat seat, see p. 223.) If so, lower the seat first and then proceed with the flat seat alteration.

FAST FIT SOLUTION

On the back pattern piece, lower the bottom of the crotch curve slightly, maintaining the original crotch point.

STEP-BY-STEP SOLUTION

1 On the pattern, trace your size with a highlighter pen.

2 On the back pattern piece, a few inches in from the crotch point, lower the crotch curve $\frac{1}{4}$ in. to $\frac{1}{2}$ in. (6mm to 1.3cm). Be conservative the first time you make this adjustment; you can always lower the crotch curve more if you feel the initial amount wasn't enough.

3 Redraw the cutting line for the bottom of the crotch curve, maintaining the upper slope and returning to the original cutting line at the crotch point.

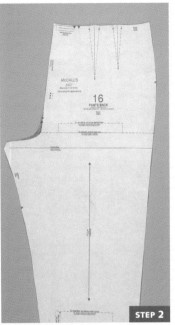

If you have a low derriere, your pants will be more comfortable and flattering if you drop the crotch curve in the lower portion ¼ in. to ½ in. (6mm to 1.3cm).

COMFY CROTCH SEAMS

Crotch seams that are sewn in a horseshoe shape allow pants to hang better and are more comfortable to wear. After sewing all darts, pleats and the zipper, sew each leg separately, both the inner and the outer legs. Then turn one leg right side out, and insert the right side out leg into the wrong side out leg. The shape of the crotch seam now looks like a horseshoe.

Sew the crotch seam from front to back. Resew the lower half of the crotch seam a second time, sewing very close to the seamline and including a bit of ¼-in. (6mm) wide twill tape as a stabilizer. To reduce bulk and create comfort, trim the lower half of the crotch seam to ¼ in. (6mm).

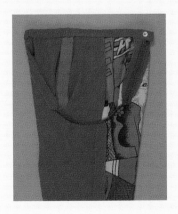

Slip one leg inside the other and sew the crotch seam in a horseshoe shape. Stabilize the lower crotch with twill tape.

FITTING TIP

For the best crotch configuration and balance, try Burda and Today's Fit from Vogue and Butterick; they seem to fit best.

Protruding Derriere

THE PROBLEM

A protruding backside causes pants to cup in under the buttocks and pulls the back of your pants down every time you take a seat. As a result, you're not only uncomfortable but probably aren't happy with the way you look from the side wearing pants. With a few alterations, your pants can be hanging freely and you'll be able to sit down comfortably. In fact, your figure will look its best in pants once they fit properly.

The reason pants ride low in the center back is because there is not enough length on the back crotch hook. The first pair you make will be a bit of an experiment to get the alteration amounts right, so I suggest using scrap fabric from your stash. (It always makes me feel good to reduce my stash and make room for new treasures.) Before starting, however, it's especially important to begin with a good pants pattern. My favorites are Vogue 7027 and Butterick 3015, which have well-shaped crotches and realistic measurements, ranging from a 34-in. to 57-in. (86cm to 145cm) hip. Buy the pattern size that corresponds to your hip measurement.

Your skirts may also be shorter at center back, caused by the protruding seat stealing fabric from the hem. Skirts and dresses with a center-back or princess seam style are much kinder to your figure than a cut-on-the-fold style, since the seams can allow you to taper in at the waist and avoid the pouch that often forms there.

FAST FIT SOLUTION

On pants, add extensions to the back inner leg seams beginning at the crotch point. If you are full behind the knees, add down to the mid-calves; if you have full calves, add all the way to the pants bottom. On skirts, add horizontally to the fullest part of the seat—either your high hip or full thighs.

STEP-BY-STEP SOLUTION

Pants

1 On the pattern, outline your size or sizes with a highlighter pen, transitioning smoothly between sizes.

2 To the back inner leg, starting at the crotch point, add ½ in. to ¾ in. (1.3cm to 1.9cm) to the amount the pants scoop down at the center back waistline. You may have to add as much as 2 in. (5cm) to get rid of the problem. To help determine how much to add, tape a 2-in. (5cm) wide paper addition onto the back inner leg seams of the pattern. On the addition, draw new cutting lines at ½ in. (5cm), increasing intervals up to 2 in. (5cm). Taper to zero about 10 in. (25.4cm) down from the crotch, unless your legs are full behind the knees; in that case, taper to zero at mid-calf. If the calves are also full, do not taper the addition at all, adding all the way to the bottom of the leg.

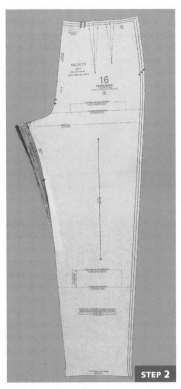

STEP 2

To add length to the crotch, add extensions to the back inner leg seams. Trace different sewing options onto the cut-out pants.

> **FITTING FACT**
> Darts can be moved, lengthened, combined into one, or divided in two—as long as they point to an area of fullness.

Protruding Derriere, *continued*

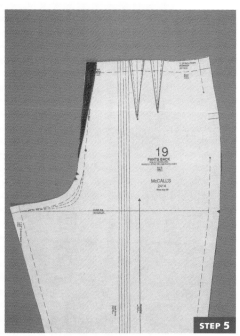

STEP 5

If your backside protrudes, you may need to taper in the center back seam or increase the size of the darts to get a smoother fit under the waistband.

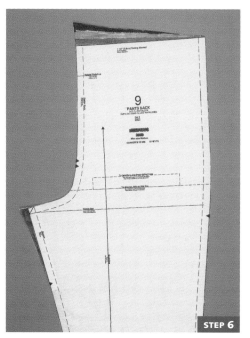

STEP 6

If an addition to the back inner leg is not enough, you may also need to add height to the center back waistline.

FITTING TIP

If your front thighs are full, you may also need to add to the front inner legs. If the front of your pants hangs free without being caught up on your front thigh, the problem is in the back only.

---

3 Cut the pants out, including all the additions on the back inner leg. Use a tracing wheel and paper to mark the seamlines on the back inner leg for all possible additions; mark the seamline on the front leg. Baste the pants together trying different combinations, matching different back seamlines to the same front seamline to see what fits best.

4 Analyze the back of the pants in a three-way mirror. If they are still cupping in under the seat, you may need to add more to the back inner leg seam.

5 Check to see if you have too much fabric under the waistband; if you have a protruding backside you may also be a bit hollow in

this area. To eliminate some of the excess fabric, add an additional back dart (if there is only one), increase the size of the darts, and taper in the center back seam.

6 If your pants still come down in the back when you sit, the waistline at center back may need extra length. Add above the waist at the center back in $1/2$-in. (1.3cm) intervals, always tapering to zero by the side seam. Try different combinations until you find the correct amount you need.

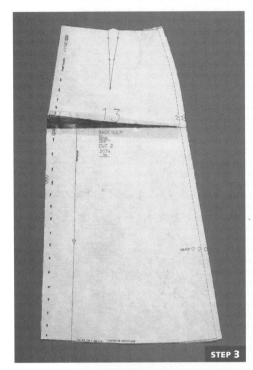

STEP 3

A protruding bottom needs more height at the center back. Cut the pattern apart horizontally, leaving the seam allowance intact to act as a hinge, and lift the center back. Hemlines will no longer be shorter at center back.

Skirts

1 On your pattern, draw a horizontal line across the fullest part of the seat—either your high hip or full thighs, whichever is the bigger measure.

2 Starting at the center back, cut the pattern apart to the side seam, leaving the side seam intact so that it can act as a hinge.

3 Spread the pattern open by the amount your skirt usually hikes up at center back. This alteration lifts the center back and causes the upper part of the skirt to tip in, which means you need to add a center back seam if there isn't one.

Full Thighs, Pants

THE PROBLEM

Pants that catch on the thighs are unflattering and uncomfortable. To draw attention to the problem, wrinkles form a "smile" right above the crotch, and every time you stand up from a seated position you need to pull down the pants legs so they hang straight. This is a constant tug-of-war as fabric gets hung up on the protruding body parts. In addition, ease intended for the back of the garment is borrowed by the front, pulling the inner leg seam forward. The result is overfitting in the back of the pants.

Switching to skirts is not your only option—try this simple alteration instead. By adding an extension to the front inner leg seam you'll have more fabric covering the problem area. The first step is to determine how much, and how far down, you need to add.

FAST FIT SOLUTION

Add anywhere from ½ in. to 1½ in. (1.3cm to 3.8cm) to the front inner leg seam, depending on the best fit. Add half the amount at the side seam to keep the legs balanced.

STEP-BY-STEP SOLUTION

1 On the pattern, use a highlighter pen to outline the size that corresponds to your measurements.

2 Add a 2-in. (5cm) wide paper extension to the front inner leg.

3 From the cutting line at the crotch tip, measure out ½ in., 1 in., and 1½ in. (1.3cm, 2.5cm, and 3.8cm).

4 Draw in new cutting lines, following the shape of the inner leg cutting line. If the fullness goes all the way to your knee (that is, there's no space between your thighs), extend

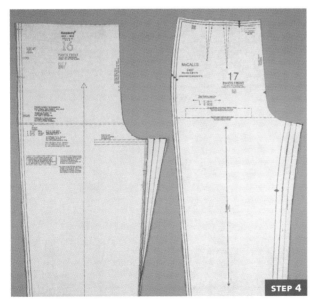

STEP 4

A fuller thigh needs an addition on the front inner leg. If your knees or calves are full, don't taper out the addition too soon.

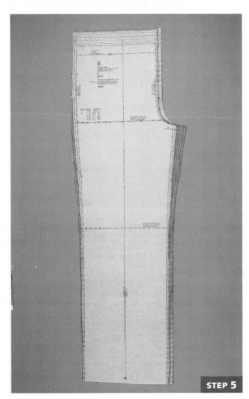

STEP 5

If you've added more than ½ in. (1.3cm) at the front inner leg, add half that amount to the outer leg for balance.

the addition 2 in. (5cm) past the bottom of the knee. If you have full calves, continue the extension all the way to the bottom of the leg. If the addition tapers off too quickly down the front leg, a new wrinkle will develop where there is not enough fullness for the pants to fall smoothly.

5 If you're adding more than ½ in. (1.3cm) onto the front inner leg, the addition must be balanced by an addition at the side seam of half the amount you are adding to the inner leg. For example, if you need 1 in. (2.5cm) at the front inner leg, make an addition of ½ in. (1.3cm) at the side seam from the full hip to the hem to keep the leg balanced.

6 Cut out your front pants pattern piece from scrap fabric with the full, 2-in. (5cm) wide extension on the inner leg. Cut out the back pattern piece using the original cutting lines. Mark the three optional seamlines that correspond to the new cutting lines you added to the front inner leg. Also mark the seamline on the back. This makes matching up the seamlines easier.

7 Sew the pants using the ½-in. (1.3cm) extended seamline. If the fit isn't as comfortable as you'd like, move out to the next seamline marked on the garment piece. Remember not to change the sewing line on the back.

SMOOTHING THE LUMPS AND BUMPS

For many women, the body silhouette from hip to lower thigh isn't a smooth, gradual curve. Instead, it's a series of hills and valleys. A neat trick I learned from a couturier house builds support into the side seams, thus giving the illusion of a smooth curve over this part of the body.

Cut a strip of 2-in. (5cm) wide Petersham or medium-weight interfacing on the bias, long enough to extend from waist to knee on both legs—about 1½ yd. (1.4m) are usually sufficient. Preshrink the Petersham by submerging it in hot water (this will prevent the side seams of your pants from drawing up if the Petersham shrinks). Don't stretch the interfacing, if you are using it, as you press.

Join the side seam of your pants and press the seam allowances open. Center the Petersham or interfacing flat over the open seam allowance, from waist to knee. Pin one edge of the interfacing to each side of the seam allowance. Machine straight stitch the edges to the seam allowances without catching the garment in the stitches. If you're using interfacing, fuse it according to the manufacturer's instructions. Apply the waistband to the pants, and you'll have a smooth fit over your upper thighs.

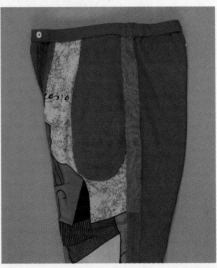

Smooth out those hills and valleys on the side seam by sewing Petersham ribbon or bias interfacing to the pressed open seam allowance from waist to knee.

Full Thighs, Dresses, and Skirts

THE PROBLEM

Full thighs can cause fitting problems in skirts as well as in pants. The appearance of horizontal wrinkles between the thighs is a good indicator. In addition, ease intended for the back of the garment is borrowed by the front, so the side seams swing forward and the garment fit may be snug across the back. Interestingly, the full thigh alteration is almost identical to that of a full hip—adding at the side seam to avoid over-fitting the area. Full calves aren't a problem because slits or kick pleats provide the necessary room for your calves. The following alteration will require some help from a friend.

FAST FIT SOLUTION

Determine the amount of additional fabric you need over the front thigh area; add accordingly to the side seams (half on each side) of the front pattern piece. Taper the extension to the original cutting line at the waist.

STEP-BY-STEP SOLUTION

1 Put on a unitard. Ask a friend to pin a piece of twill tape on each side of your body, at the correct location of the side seams. Place the tape in the middle of your leg from the ankle to the knee, then straight up to the waist. (Don't use the seamlines on the unitard as guidelines.)

2 Use a tape measure to measure across the front of your thighs, from one piece of twill tape to another. To this measurement, add the amount of movement and design ease that you want in this area of the finished garment. For fitted pants and straight skirts add 1$\frac{1}{2}$ in. (3.8cm) of ease; for pleated pants and a semi-full skirt, add 2 in. (5cm).

3 On the pattern, measure across the front pattern piece at the thighs, excluding the seam allowances. If the pattern piece instructions are to cut on the fold or to cut two, double the measurement. If you have more than one pattern piece for the front of the garment, measure the additional pieces in the same manner. Compare this number to your front thigh measurement taken in Step 2, plus ease. The difference is the amount that you need to add to the side seams of the front piece. Add fabric to the front pattern piece only.

4 Make a pattern paper extension that is half the width of the total alteration amount. Tape it to the front side seam, so that you will add half on each side.

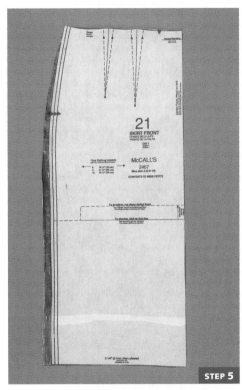

STEP 5

Full thighs call for an addition on the front pattern piece of a skirt. This helps eliminate the side seams being pulled forward and the derriere being overfitted.

||||||||||||||||||||||||||||||||||||||||||||||||||||||||||||||||||||||||||||||||||||||||||||||||||||||||||||||||||||||||||||

ADDING PLEATS

Protruding thighs are best camou-flaged in pleated pants or skirts be-cause the pleat releases in time to give added fabric over the protruding front thigh. If your pattern doesn't already in-clude pleats, it's an easy matter to add them in yourself. A pleat can be added to pants or a skirt simply by cutting the pattern apart on the grain from the waist to the hem. Spread the pattern apart 2 in. (5cm)—the width of a typical front pleat at the waist—tapering the spread to zero by the hem. If your full-ness extends into the knee, widen the spread as it approaches the bottom.

If the pattern has a dart, the pleat can incorporate the dart width; you sew a pleat rather than a dart. Or if the pattern has existing pleats, they can be made deeper, giving more fabric over the upper thigh. (For proper pleat location, see "Crease Line Positioning" on p. 203.) Pleats hang better if they are supported by ending the stitch line at the pleat fold rather than at the end of the pleat.

Begin sewing at the top of the pleat. Instead of ending the sewing line at the end of the pleat, continue sewing, angling up ½ in. (1.3cm) to end your sewing line at the fold.

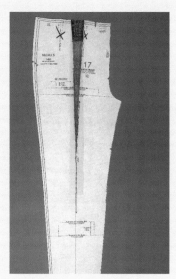

Increasing the pleat width or adding a pleat are good solutions for protruding front thighs.

||||||||||||||||||||||||||||||||||||||||||||||||||||||||||||||||||||||||||||||||||||||||||||||||||||||||||||||||||||||||||||

5 Draw a new cutting line from the high hip to the bottom of the hem allowance. Taper the extension width to the original cutting line at the waist, unless there's a big difference (more than two sizes) between your waist and hip size. In this case, taper in two sizes at the waist and, if necessary, increase the width of darts and pleats.

Full Calves

THE PROBLEM

Thanks to slitted skirts, full calves aren't generally a problem when it comes to skirts. Pants, however, are another matter entirely. If you have full calves, your pants tend to get hung up on the calf and wrinkle under the seat. If your calves protrude farther than your backside, it can be difficult to get the pants to hang off of the backside without catching on the calf.

A very full style pants allows the pants to fall freely, no matter what curves are underneath. Another option is at the other end of the spectrum—a very snug fitting pants in a stretch fabric actually helps minimize the problem, because there's no extra fabric to catch on the calf. Since the problem is usually caused by fullness in the back, the following alteration adds to the back inner leg.

FAST FIT SOLUTION

Make a small addition to the back inner leg, tapering to the original cutting line just above the knee.

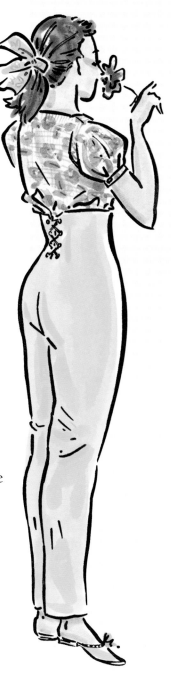

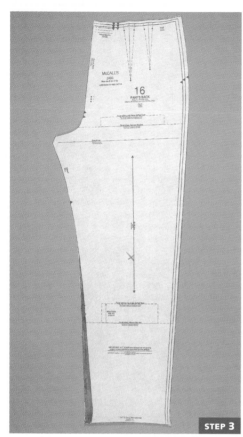

STEP 3

Full calves need an addition on the back inner leg.

STEP-BY-STEP SOLUTION

1 Measure your calves at their fullest part.

2 Take a flat pattern measure of the front and back pants legs in the calf area. While the amount of fullness is up to the individual, I prefer at least 2 in. (5cm) of ease to prevent the pants from getting hung up on the calf.

3 On the back pattern piece, tape tissue paper to the inner and outer leg from 2 in. (5cm) above the knee down. Starting at the bottom of the pants, add ⅜ in. to ¾ in. (1cm to 1.9cm) to the back inner leg. Draw in a new cutting line, tapering it out and making the addition on the back inner leg. Taper back to the original cutting line 1 in. (2.5cm) above the knee.

4 If your addition is more than ¾ in. (1.9cm), both inner and outer leg seams can be let out from the knee down.

Uneven Hemlines

THE PROBLEM

Uneven hemlines can be caused by a number of things, including posture, a waistline that slopes up or down, or a high hip. A protruding stomach or backside or a very full bust can also result in uneven hemlines. A good look in the mirror will help you identify the problem.

No matter what the cause, the result is the same: an uneven hemline. With the help of a 60-in (15m) long T-square, you can determine just how much the hem hikes up or droops down. The following instructions can also be used to even out the hem on a garment you've already made.

FAST FIT SOLUTION

Put on the garment that has an uneven hemline and use a T-square to measure the desired length (distance from the floor) all the way around the bottom of the garment. Place pins at the desired location and cut off anything below the pins.

STEP-BY-STEP SOLUTION

1 Put on the garment that needs altering.

2 Using the T-square, position the horizontal line of the T on the floor with the vertical portion of the T sticking up. With the help of a friend, place pins around the garment, equidistant from the floor at the desired length. For example, if you want the finished length of your jacket to be 24 in. (61cm)–30 in. (76cm) above the floor—move the T-square around the

STEP 2

Uneven hemlines are often caused by posture. T-squares are useful for determining the alteration amount. With the T-square on the floor, measure both front and back lengths. The difference is the amount that must be added to create an even hemline.

body, placing pins 30 in. (76cm) from the floor all around the jacket.

3 Cut off anything below the pins. This exercise helps determine how much you'll need to subtract for your next garment.

4 If a protruding tummy or posture is causing the problem, use the T-square to calculate the difference between the floor measurements to the center front and center back; add this amount above the front waistline.

5 Taper off the addition by the side seam and add to the front facing. If your garment has a waistline seam, the alteration is made at the seamline.

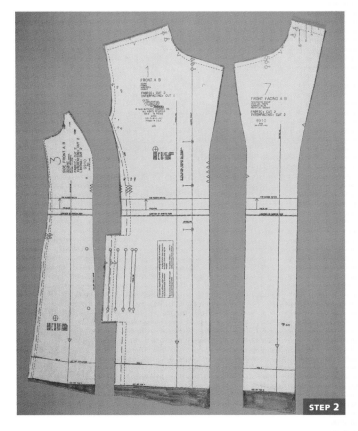

STEP 2

If your jacket hikes up in front, lengthen the front, front facing, and side front, blending to the original cutting line at the side seam.

Pattern List

If you would like to sew your own version of a garment pictured in this book, the following is a list of the patterns that Sandra used.

Jacket: Butterick 3013;
Skirt: Vogue 3333
(see p. 3)

Vogue 7396
(see p. 50)

Vogue 7263 (see p. 75)

Jacket: Vogue 7334;
Skirt: Vogue 7333
(see p. 1)

Jacket: Vogue 7334;
Pants: purchased
pleated microfiber
from Babette
(800-677-7246)
(see p. 3)

Jacket: Vogue 7360;
Skirt: Vogue 7333
(see p. 3)

Dress: Vogue 7257;
Vest: Butterick 3016
(see p. 2)

Vogue 7360
(see p. 119)

Discontinued
New Look Pattern 6259
(see p. 2)

Vogue 7281
(see p. 119)

Top and Pants:
Vogue 7397
(see p. 2)

Vogue 7136
(see p. 120)

Vogue 7136
(see p. 121)

Index